Consultation and Cultural Heritage

LET US REASON TOGETHER

This book is dedicated to my mother and sister,
who did not take "no" for an answer, and to Shorty, the best
negotiator I know as he always gets what he wants.

Claudia Nissley

To the memory of Robert R. Garvey, Jr., who taught me to consult and
provided object lessons in how it's done.

Thomas F. King

Consultation and Cultural Heritage

LET US REASON TOGETHER

Claudia Nissley

Thomas F. King

Left Coast
Press inc.

Walnut Creek, California

LEFT COAST PRESS, INC.
1630 North Main Street, #400
Walnut Creek, CA 94596
http://www.LCoastPress.com

ISBN 978-1-61132-398-6   hardcover
ISBN 978-1-61132-399-3   paperback
ISBN 978-1-61132-778-6   institutional eBook
ISBN 978-1-61132-744-1   consumer eBook

Library of Congress Cataloging-in-Publication Data
Nissley, Claudia.
  Consultation and cultural heritage : let us reason together / Claudia Nissley, Thomas F. King.
      pages cm
  Includes bibliographical references and index.
  ISBN 978-1-61132-398-6 (hardback : alk. paper) -- ISBN 978-1-61132-399-3 (pbk. : alk. paper) -- ISBN 978-1-61132-778-6 (institutional ebook) -- ISBN 978-1-61132-744-1 (consumer ebook)
  1. Cultural property--Conservation and restoration. 2. Environmental protection--Management. 3. Interagency coordination. 4. Intergovernmental cooperation. I. King, Thomas F. II. Title.
  CC35.N57 2014
  363.6'9--dc23
                                            2013041553

Printed in the United States of America

♾™ The paper used in this publication meets the minimum requirements of American National Standard for Information Sciences—Permanence of Paper for Printed Library Materials, ANSI/NISO Z39.48–1992.

CONTENTS

PREFACE

The authors of this book have spent roughly (sometimes very roughly) seventy collective years working with the U.S. historic preservation and environmental laws that require "consultation." Over the decades, we've gained some notion of what consultation ought to entail, and what often happens to it instead. We've learned about what works and what doesn't.

Until recently, we weren't sure that a book about consultation was needed. Quite a few books, journal articles and government guidelines that touch on it, like education, psychology, and law. There are books collaborative planning, dispute resolution, mediation, and facilitation. A sampling of these sources is provided in our bibliography. In the 1980s and 90s we took part in enough seemingly satisfactory—or at least not much contested—consultations to have been lulled into thinking that the principles of consultation were pretty widely understood and that its practice was improving.

In the twenty-first century, though, we've been startled at what some agencies of government have come to think of as consultation; it's as though the concept has become foreign to the thinking of those charged with doing it. Often, consultation seems to be regarded as merely an administrative task, to be endured and checked off a list of "things to do" before taking an action already decided upon. This is a waste of everyone's time and money, and inconsistent with what we think, and in some cases know, to have been the intent of the laws.

So for better or worse—since there seems to be nothing else we can do about it—we decided that a book would be in order, and here it is. Recognizing that it will be used by busy people in working environments, we've tried to make it something other than an academic tome; this was easy, since neither of us is an academic. We've tried to keep it short and straightforward. Those who want to explore the subject in more detail, or along more theoretical lines, can find avenues to pursue in the references.

Claudia Nissley and Thomas F. King, "Preface" in *Consultation and Cultural Heritage: Let Us Reason Together,* pp. 7-8. © 2014 Left Coast Press, Inc. All rights reserved.

Acknowledgements

Although no one but us is responsible for our errors and omissions, people have advised us, shared information, and commented on drafts. Kathleen Schamel and Douglas Pulak of the U.S. Department of Veterans Affairs, David Moore of Hardy Heck Moore in Austin, Texas, and Katy Coyle and Kate Kuranda of R. C. Goodwin & Associates have been invaluable colleagues in recent consultations, while Mary Orton, Glenn Knowles, and Beverly Hefernan made possible the Grand Canyon fish removal consultation discussed in Chapter 7. Kurt Dongoske, Tribal Historic Preservation Officer for the Pueblo of Zuni, was a treasured colleague in that consultation, too, and advised about the Amity Pueblo case discussed in Chapter 3. Judith Innes and David Booher of the University of California, Berkeley and the Center for Collaborative Policy shared the wisdom they have gained from a generation of practice and theorizing in collaborative reasoning-together, while Kerry Kirk Pflugh and Suzanne Shannon of the New Jersey Department of Environmental Protection shared their comparative analysis of public participation methods—now, sadly, rather hard to find. Alex Bauer of Queens College provided valuable insights into the Gezi Park case in Istanbul. Hugh McCann advised about what God really meant in Isaiah 1:18. Charles Eccleston, Ray Clark, and Owen Schmidt have helped us understand how consultation happens (or doesn't) under the National Environmental Policy Act. Kurt Russo, Nora McDowell, Reba Fuller, Robert Van Zile, Linda Otero and many others have shared American Indian tribal perspectives on consultation, and Elizabeth Bradshaw of Rio Tinto has helped us visualize the importance of consultation from the perspective of international extractive industries. Colleagues at the U.S. Advisory Council on Historic Preservation, Department of Veterans Affairs, General Services Administration, and Departments of Agriculture, Defense and Interior as well as in many State Historic Preservation Offices have contributed to our understanding of government perspectives. Kelley Hays-Gilpin of Northern Arizona University helped us locate the cover image (of people with hands waving in the air) from Baja California's Cueva Pintada; Bob Mark and Evelyn Billo of Rupestrian Cyber Services provided it. And of course, our greatest thanks go to Mitch Allen and his colleagues at Left Coast Press—Jennifer Collier, Katie Peña, Louise Bell, Lisa Devenish, and Sally Gregg, for making this book possible.

CHAPTER 1

Introduction

Come, let us reason together. — ISAIAH 1:18

Why This Book?

"Consultation" is the legally mandated duty of many organizations that build things and manage land in the United States and other countries (c.f. Nissley 2011). Environmental and historic preservation laws, among others, require it—sometimes with scientists and other experts, sometimes with specified governmental authorities, sometimes with indigenous groups like American Indian tribes, sometimes with local communities, occasionally with the general public. Executive orders and regulations add specificity to the requirements.

What does this mean? What is "consultation" supposed to accomplish, and how is it supposed to be done? The laws and regulations are mostly silent about such details.

The Word

We *consult* a dictionary to find out what a word means. We *consult* a physician to find out what ails us. We *consult* a lawyer to file bankruptcy. This kind of one-way consultation—just seeking and getting advice from a selected consultant—cannot be what the various legal authorities mean by consultation. Consider some examples:

U.S. National Historic Preservation Act, Section 110(a)(2)
(16 U.S.C. § 470h-2(a-2))

> Each Federal agency shall establish...a preservation program...[which]... shall ensure...that the agency's preservation-related activities are carried

out in *consultation* with other Federal, State, and local agencies, Indian tribes, Native Hawaiian organizations...and...the private sector [emphasis added].

U.S. National Environmental Policy Act, Section 102 (42 U.S.C. § 4332)

The Congress authorizes and directs that...all agencies of the Federal Government shall...identify and develop methods and procedures, *in consultation* with the Council on Environmental Quality...,which will insure that presently unquantified environmental amenities and values may be given appropriate consideration in decisionmaking along with economic and technical considerations;...[and]...shall *consult with* and obtain the comments of any Federal agency which has jurisdiction by law or special expertise with respect to any environmental impact involved [emphasis added].

U.S. Native American Graves Protection and Repatriation Act, Section 5(b) (25 CFR § 3003)

The inventories and identifications required under subsection (a) shall be... completed *in consultation* with tribal government and Native Hawaiian organization officials and traditional religious leaders [emphasis added].

United Nations Declaration on the Rights of Indigenous Peoples (UNDRIP), Article 19 (United Nations 2007)

States shall *consult* and cooperate in good faith with the indigenous peoples concerned through their own representative institutions in order to obtain their free, prior and informed consent before adopting and implementing legislative or administrative measures that may affect them [emphasis added].

UNDRIP, Article 38

States shall *consult* and cooperate in good faith with the indigenous peoples concerned through their own representative institutions in order to obtain their free and informed consent prior to the approval of any project affecting their lands or territories and other resources, particularly in connection with the development, utilization or exploitation of mineral, water or other resources [emphasis added].

Secretariat of the Convention on Biological Diversity, *Akwé: Kon* **Guidelines (SCBD 2004)**

The sponsor of a development proposal or the responsible government authority should engage in a process of notification and *public consultation* of intention to carry out a development. Such notification should use all normal public means of notification (print, electronic and personal media, including newspapers, radio, television, mailings, village/town meetings, etc.), take into account the situation of remote or isolated and largely non-literate communities, and ensure that such notification and consultation take place in the language(s) of the communities and region that will be affected [emphasis added].

African Development Bank: *Handbook on Stakeholder Consultation and Participation* **(ADB 2001)**

Consultation (comprises): 1. Information-sharing: dissemination of documents, public meetings, information seminars; 2. Listening and learning: field visits, interviews, consultative meetings; 3. Joint assessment: participatory needs assessment, beneficiary assessments [emphasis added].

What these and innumerable other laws, regulations, executive orders, policy papers, and guidelines are referring to when they say to "consult" or to engage in "consultation" is clearly something more than the equivalent of a visit to the doctor or lawyer, or thumbing through a dictionary. It's something much more organic and interactive— an ongoing, flexible process designed to exchange views. But it must surely go beyond the exchange of views alone. What point is there in exchanging views if there isn't the intent to do something *with* those views, to *accomplish* something?

It seems so obvious that it ought to go without saying, and mostly does: consultation under the environmental, historic preservation, and related laws is literally about *reasoning together*—thinking through a problem or set of problems and seeking a solution.

Maybe because it *does* usually go without saying, the intent and meaning of consultation seems to have been lost on a lot of those charged with doing it. In many of the U.S. government "consultations" we've participated in or been aware of recently, the outcome has been pretty much predetermined. Someone is going to build or permit X project at location A, or use Y parcel of land for B purposes. That someone, or that someone's overseeing regulator, will listen to what you the stakeholders (Indian tribes, property owners, environmental groups, just plain citizens) have to say, nod their heads sagely and promise to think about it, and then check off the "consultation" box on their spreadsheet and go ahead. As a stakeholder engaged in the consultation process, if you don't like it, you may sue them if you can afford the lawyers.

This, we want to say unequivocally, is *not* what we think consultation ought to be, or what the laws, regulations, and guidelines intend—or what makes sense for a government agency or anyone else to do. What we think the legal and other authorities *do* intend, and how to make good on that intent, are what this book is about.

Simple Notions

There's nothing complicated about what we'll be discussing—indeed a lot of what we recommend is blazingly obvious. What we've found in our own practices, though, and in the classes we teach for government agencies, consulting firms, and others, is that somehow, when people get into government and industry and start making or supporting decisions about whether and how to do things that affect the public, they fall into strange patterns of thought and behavior. The obvious principles of effective human interaction that most of us learn as children and have reinforced through our adult lives somehow don't get applied to their work as professionals and public officials. A book may not be the best way to encourage re-connection with those principles, but it's the one that's available to us, so here it is.

Some Conventions

Although we hope this book will be useful to a wide variety of people engaged in (or wanting to engage in) consultation under environmental and cultural resource laws and regulations, we've directed it toward people, corporations, and agencies responsible for setting up and doing consultation—generally the sponsors of land-use and development projects that require review under the laws, and the government agencies that oversee them.

Our focus is on consultation that takes place under the laws and regulations of the United States and its political subdivisions (states, local governments), because that's the arena in which we have had most of our experience. But we've tried to make this book as relevant as we can to people working in other countries, and we think a lot of what we have to say is just common sense, applicable everywhere.

There are some terms we use conventionally in talking about consultation under the U.S. laws—some more or less specialized, some more common but with more or less special definitions. We've provided a glossary as Appendix 1, but in the interests of clarity there are a few terms we need to define at the outset.

Agency: In most if not all reviews conducted under laws like the National Environmental Policy Act (NEPA) and the National Historic Preservation Act (NHPA), an agency of the United States government is a central player. They're usually the ones responsible for making sure the review happens, either because they're proposing the action or because they're considering assisting or permitting it. In other legal contexts (e.g., state, tribal, and local law in the United States and the laws of other nations), an agency may be part of some other sort of governmental body. Whatever the particulars, it's this sort of proponent or overseeing government entity that we usually mean when we use the term agency. If we mean a specific agency, we'll give it a real or apocryphal name. We'll often refer to the responsible agency, meaning the agency responsible for carrying out the Environmental Impact Assessment (EIA) or a Cultural Resource Management (CRM) review; we do not mean to imply that such agencies always (or often) behave responsibly.

Consulting party: "Consulting party" is a commonly used term of art under NHPA Section 106; in that context it means someone—an individual, organization, agency, tribe—who consults about a project that's under review. We use the term more broadly here, but with a consistent meaning: anybody who consults or is consulted, or who ought to consult or be consulted, under any legal authority (or under no authority at all). A consultant, (like either of the authors) may be a consulting party, but a consulting party is not necessarily a consultant.

Cultural Resource Management (CRM): This term of art is widely used in the United States, and increasingly in Australia, some African countries, and elsewhere, to refer to a set of laws, regulations, and practices designed to manage the cultural aspects of the environment and to control impacts on those aspects. The term "cultural heritage management," or just "cultural heritage," is used elsewhere, and sometimes in the United States, to mean roughly the same thing. We use the term as King defined it in *A Companion to Cultural Resource Management* (King 2011, 2):

> "Cultural resources" are all the aspects of the physical and supra-physical environment that human beings and their societies value for reasons having to do with culture. Included are culturally valued sites, buildings, and other places, plants and animals, atmospheric phenomena, sights and sounds, artifacts and other objects, documents, traditions, arts, crafts, ways of life, means of expression and systems of belief. "Cultural Resource Management" means actions undertaken to manage such phenomena, or—importantly—to identify and manage the ways in which change affects or may affect them.

Many people and government agencies define the term more narrowly, and for purposes of this book the definition doesn't greatly matter; just understand that when we talk about consulting in "CRM," we're talking about consulting under laws, regulations, and practices dealing with some aspect or aspects of the cultural environment.

Environmental Impact Assessment (EIA). By EIA we mean the laws, regulations, and practices involved in assessing the impacts of projects and proposals on the natural and cultural environments. In the United States EIA is performed under the authority of the NEPA, state, and tribal NEPA equivalents, and a number of related legal authorities. In other nations and in the context of international development, EIA is performed under a range of national and international laws, treaties, regional understandings, United Nations mandates, and funding agency rules.

Project: When we use the term "project," we're referring to whatever kind of project is subjected to review under the EIA and CRM laws and regulations. Examples from our own experience over the last few years include but are not limited to:

- Development of wind and solar energy projects;
- Redevelopment of medical facilities for military veterans;
- Development of mines and quarries;
- Management of wild horses and burros;
- Remediation of toxic waste sites;
- Construction of highway interchanges, railroads, and multimodal transit facilities; and
- Disposal of government facilities no longer needed for their original purposes.

Review: Most times when we use the word "review," we mean the review of a proposed project's effects on the environment, or some aspect of the environment, under one or more laws or regulations.

Sponsor or Proponent: The sponsor, or proponent, of a project is, of course, the entity that proposes to make it happen—often a government agency, sometimes a corporation or other business entity, occasionally an individual.

You: Exactly who we mean when we use the word "you"—as we do a great deal—depends on the context in which we use it. Often we're talking to the person or people responsible for consulting on behalf of a project sponsor or an oversight agency. In some cases we're talking to those consulting on behalf of some other stakeholder—an Indian tribe or other indigenous group, an affected community, a citizens' group, a local government, property owners, or whoever else may need and want to consult. We try to be clear in each case about just who we mean by "you."

For other terms and acronyms, please see Appendix 1.

What Do We Consult About?

In our personal lives, we consult all the time. We consult with spouses about whether to buy new cars or new houses, or how to take care of sick children and pets. We consult with colleagues about joint projects. We consult with friends about where and when to go fishing. Government agencies and private corporations consult about a lot of things, too, but the focus of this book is on the consultation that's done when projects are being planned that may affect the environment. That's when the various EIA, CRM, and historic or heritage preservation laws and regulations kick in, requiring consultation, sometimes with specific groups and sometimes with the public in general.

Under those laws and regulations, if you're planning a project of some kind you characteristically have to—or at least ought to—consult with people at the following more or less specific points in the planning process:

1. **Formulation:** When you're first formulating the idea for the project, you ought to do at least some consultation to help decide whether it's going to fly, or run into such a buzz-saw of opposition that you'd be smarter to pursue an alternative. Few laws really require consultation at this stage, however, and it's rarely done—which probably leads to a lot of wasted time and money. Right now in the United States, for example, there's a great clamor to open up federal land for the development of industrial-scale wind and solar energy; the president himself has directed that such projects be "green-lighted." But many such projects are proposed in environmentally sensitive areas, and areas that Indian tribes believe to be spiritually powerful and culturally significant. They may be great projects, but everyone might have an easier time with them if they'd consult just a bit with those who may be affected by them, before committing themselves to getting them built.

2. **Scoping:** Once we get the project more or less defined—you think we want to put in a dilithium mine somewhere in Poverty County, Utazona, because that's where the ore is—you begin to think about what its environmental impacts might be and how to control them. Or maybe you, assuming "you" are the moguls planning to finance the mine, don't think about those impacts, but your lawyers tell you that others will, so you'd better get your ducks in a row. At this point you ought to engage in what some of the regulations call "scoping"—figuring out the scope of work you'll have to perform, or have performed, in order to characterize the project's likely impacts and figure out what to do about them. You ought now to consult with whatever government agencies may be involved, and with the people who live, work, worship, or recreate in the

area or areas that may be affected, to see what they think you ought to do. Yes, some of them may say "get lost" or worse, but it's better to find this out now, rather than later. It's at this point—if not earlier—that you should start consulting with any indigenous groups with cultural or other connections to the potentially affected area, which in the United States means not only Indian tribes whose current reservations will be affected, but such tribes (as well as Native Hawaiians, Samoans, or whoever else may be indigenous to our area) that now live elsewhere but used to have ties to your area. In the United States, despite regulations that pretty explicitly call for consultative scoping, it seldom seems to happen, and that causes a lot of trouble. On those energy projects we just mentioned, it's standard procedure for the overseeing federal agency—usually the Bureau of Land Management in the Department of the Interior—to tell the project sponsors to hire archaeologists to go find all the "sites," and then plan their solar arrays or wind generators to "avoid" them. A tribe or a local environmental group may have very strong feelings about the landscape in which those "sites" lie (or don't lie), and about whether what they value there can be taken care of through physical "avoidance," but they're not consulted in establishing the scope of work for identifying "historic properties" or "cultural resources," and they're left with no option but to hire lawyers and sue. That's a waste of everyone's time, money, and patience.

3. **Data gathering and analysis:** As you carry out your scope of work— that is, as you perform the work decided on during scoping to figure out what may be affected by your project, or have this work performed by contractors—the idea is to try to determine what alternatives might accomplish the project's purposes and what the effects of those alternatives may be. That is what the assessment of environmental impacts means. This is where it's all too common for a government agency or project sponsor to just "send in the biologists," or archaeologists, or whatever technical specialists they're led to believe are likely to be relevant, to look for endangered species or ancient artifacts. That's fine as far as it goes, but it's very, very important to engage the potentially affected people at this point. They, and the aspects of the environment that are important to them, are critical to your planning. It's they who

can tell you what the environment looks like to *them*, and what it is about your plans that bother them—or that they like. Getting them involved in developing the data on which your analysis of alternatives and environmental impacts will be based, and in the analysis itself, can pay big dividends. In cases we've worked on where Indian tribes and local communities were invited to be partners in the identification and analysis of impacts, consultation has usually proceeded smoothly. Actually, though, we're seldom brought in on such cases; we mostly are called on (by one side or another) to help with cases where affected communities have *not* been involved, and expensive conflicts have arisen at the last minute.

4. **Making decisions:** Once you have a handle on what the effects of the project are likely to be, and what alternatives may be feasible, then the project sponsor and the regulatory agencies overseeing the work try to reach decisions about whether and how to proceed. Consultation with all concerned and affected parties now ought to focus on this question: should this project proceed, given its likely impacts, and if so, under what conditions and with what sorts of measures to mitigate the impacts? This is the point at which you're likely to want to reach and document a formal agreement (see Chapter 6), although you may have reached what amounted to interim agreements earlier, for example, on the scope of EIA. With respect to impacts on historic places under NHPA, this is the step at which everybody sits down and tries to negotiate a formal memorandum of agreement (MOA).

5. **Implementation:** Finally, it's usually necessary and appropriate to consult as the project is implemented, if it's implemented—to make sure things stay on track, to resolve any conflicts that arise, and to address any changes that have to be made in what's been agreed upon. Some MOAs under NHPA include substantial provisions for such ongoing consultation, specifying meetings and plan reviews at, say, 35, 50, and 75 percent design stages. Some provide for cooperative monitoring of progress in carrying out the terms of the agreement, and almost all include specific procedures for conflict resolution.

Of course, it's not necessarily, or even very often, a simple five-step process. Consultation is best carried out as an organic, flexible, adaptive process that begins when the project is a gleam in somebody's eye and continues until the dilithium runs out and the mine is closed (a process that will also need consultation). And each step in the process may include multiple sub-steps. It's very often necessary to stop and reconsider, perhaps change course, particularly when gathering and analyzing data and when making decisions. Each of these sub-steps may require, or benefit from, consultation.

However and whenever we consult, the process involves some basic, pretty simple principles and procedures. These are what we explore in the chapters to come.

CHAPTER 2

What Is Consultation and What Is It For?

Consultation and "Public Participation"

There is some tendency among government agencies and consulting firms to confuse consultation with "public participation"—on which there's a large literature and a considerable range of standard procedures (c.f. Bejerle 2002; CEAA 2012; Dietz & Stern 2008; Environmental Agency 2010; EPA n.d.; Innes & Booher 2010; Kaner et al. 2007; NRC 2008). Consultation is one way that the public, or various publics, participate in government planning, but the two terms are not synonyms. Public participation is a broad term, encompassing a tremendous range of activities, but it doesn't necessarily have a purpose. If a government agency is absolutely, 100 percent committed to doing something—say, putting up a building at a specific location—and it holds a public meeting about it, receives public input, and then goes on with construction, it's engaged in public participation but it has not engaged on consultation. Consultation, as we'll see, is a more collegial process, a two (or more) way conversation that's somehow aimed at reaching a meeting of the minds. Such public participation activities as holding public hearings or meetings and publishing notices seeking public comments may be *parts* of a consultation process, but they aren't consultation in themselves. On the other hand, public participation can involve a great deal *more* than consultation, including building a community's capacity to participate in decision making, often over long periods of time, and complex, multi-party deliberations. So consultation is often a part of public participation, but is not necessarily all there is to the participation process.

Consultation and "Collaborative Rationality"

Judith Innes and David Booher, in various writings but especially in their 2010 book, *Planning With Complexity,* offer many of the same criticisms we do of traditional government planning, and offer a very hopeful alternative model, which they call "collaborative rationality." Collaborative rationality involves a deeply interactive program of – well, consultation among multiple parties confronted with some "wicked problem," like regional water resource management, to arrive at solutions that—at least roughly—meet everyone's needs. The Innes/Booher model is very much worth careful study and consideration, but sadly, it doesn't apply very well to the bulk of the cases in which "consultation" is prescribed by the various laws and regulations. Innes and Booher are careful to stipulate that collaborative rationality is feasible only where the parties involved are not somehow interdependent—each depending (or potentially depending) on others for the solution to some sort of problem. This condition seldom exists in the consultation cases with which we are familiar. Project sponsors may depend on government regulators and land managers, but are usually in a position to impose their will on local residents, indigenous groups, and other interest groups. These groups, conversely, are not dependent on the project sponsor; typically, they just wish the sponsor would go away. That said, there is much to be learned from Innes and Booher, not the least being the light they throw on why so many consultations fail to satisfy most of those who participate.

The Basic Components of Consultation

So what is consultation? According to one of the very few U.S. government regulations that actually defines the term, it has four components, around which we'll build most of this book.

The definition is found in the regulations governing review of federal agency impacts on historic places under the National Historic Preservation Act, published by the U.S. Advisory Council on Historic Preservation (ACHP). It goes like this:

> Consultation *means the process of seeking, discussing, and considering the views of other participants, and, where feasible, seeking agreement with them* [emphasis added]. (36 CFR §800.16(f))

Let's think about those words for a moment. What do they mean?

Seeking: looking around, asking around, finding out who the responsible agency or project sponsor should talk with, asking them what they think.

Discussing: a back and forth dialogue about whatever it is that's the subject of consultation. Does everybody like it? No? Who doesn't and why not? What can be done to make things better? Oh, that doesn't do the job? Well, what about this other option? You want X? Well, we can't do that for the following reasons, but how about if we do Y? And so on.

Considering: giving real, meaningful thought to what people say. How may it affect the sponsor's plans? How *should* it affect those plans? How can the sponsor or the overseeing agency balance it against other factors that must influence those plans—cost, feasibility, timing, other people's interests, environmental effects? What might be changed in the design or proposal to accommodate people's concerns ?

Where feasible, seeking agreement: trying to negotiate an agreement that leaves everyone reasonably satisfied—with the understanding that success is not guaranteed, and the laws, on the whole, don't require that agreement be *reached*, only that it be *sought* (and in many cases, not even that). It's implicit that this seeking should be done fairly and responsibly, though the ACHP regulations don't come right out and say so.

Though there are some tricky words in it—which we'll discuss in subsequent chapters—the ACHP definition seems to us like a good outline of what consultation ought to entail, whether we're consulting about impacts on historic places, endangered species, water or air quality, land use, or just about anything else.

But Why Bother?

But why consult at all? If you're the project sponsor or responsible agency and know what you want to do (as sponsors, at least, almost always do), and you've got the legal authority and the money to do it (less certain, but let's assume), why go out of your way to find people to talk to? Why talk to them, and consider what they say, and most of all seek agreement with them? Why bother?

And if you're not the project sponsor—if you're someone who will be affected by the project if it happens, like a neighborhood association, a property owner, a tribe—why should you trouble yourself to consult? Why spend your precious time and money engaging in an exercise that you have no reason to think will be more than just that—an exercise—and will have little or no impact on the project?

For the sponsor and agency, sure, the law, regulations, guidelines, or standards say you ought to, or even have to, but they seldom tell you *how*, and even if they do, nobody's likely to stick you with doing it in any particular way. Even the ACHP, whose regulations set forth the definition we just quoted and dissected, doesn't put much of a squeeze on anybody to consult the way the regulations indicate. You can probably get by if you just send out a public notice, have a meeting, and ignore the results. Why actually *consult*?

And if you're a tribe, a citizens group, a property owner, why consult if you're sure—based on direct experience or what you've heard and read—that the sponsor or the ostensibly responsible agency *is* just going to ignore whatever you tell them?

Two "Dead Good Reasons"

Back in 1975 Video Arts, a production company in Great Britain, put out a video called "Decisions, Decisions"—an entertaining guide to decision making for business executives (Video Arts 1975). It starred the comedian John Cleese playing various roles, including that of Her Britannic Majesty Queen Elizabeth I. Her Majesty (accurately or not) was portrayed as a strong proponent of consultation, and she said she had two "dead good reasons":

1. Through consultation you may learn things you didn't know, hadn't considered, that really ought to influence your decision; and

2. Whatever the decision you make, people are more likely to accept it, not rise up in revolt, if they feel they've had a voice in its making.

Simple, obvious, but Her Majesty's advice *does* assume a couple of characteristics of mind that may not often be found among royals—or, unfortunately, among government officials in general. If you're working for the project sponsor or overseeing agency, you ought to try to develop these characteristics:

1. Recognize that the sponsor or agency doesn't necessarily have all the answers; and

2. Consider whether maybe it's desirable—from the sponsor's or agency's point of view—for people to accept what's decided. There's some historical evidence that just rolling over people doesn't work very well, at least in the long run.

Guidance from Galilee

Most of us should be wise enough to realize that we don't have all the answers, and that things work better if we have consensus than if everybody's at one another's throats. We develop this wisdom by having acted on poorly informed decisions, observing others do so, or by having things we objected to done to us without our consent. This brings us to a principle that everyone engaged in consultation ought to keep in mind; it was articulated as a general rule of human behavior a couple of thousand years ago by a reformer of the time who's still quoted a lot today, notably by politicians:

> Therefore all things whatsoever ye would that men should do to you, do ye even so to them. —*Jesus of Nazareth, according to Matthew 7:12*

Or in its common simplified form: "Do unto others as you would have them do unto you."

In preparing to consult about something—particularly if you're a government or industry official responsible for designing and carrying out the consultation process—you'd do well to think about how *you* would want to be consulted if someone with power were planning something potentially affecting *you*. Ask yourself, for example:

- Would I be satisfied getting a letter saying, "We're planning to do XYZ; if you have any comments, please send them in within 30 days?"

- Would it be OK with me for the responsible authority to take my comments, task somebody with writing dismissive responses to them, and ignoring them?

- Would I think it reasonable for the overseeing government agency to establish in advance, unilaterally or with the project sponsor, what could and couldn't be discussed in the course of consultation?

- Would it be helpful for the responsible authority to send low-level employees or contractors to chat with me, who couldn't do a thing to accommodate my concerns?
- Would I be satisfied with "listening sessions" that collected my concerns but didn't engage me in trying to do anything about them?

No? Probably not. But all the above (and other things just as ineffective and demeaning to others) are things that government agencies and project sponsors routinely do under the guise of "consultation."

So project sponsors and government overseers would, we think, be wise to consider Queen Elizabeth's dicta and the Golden Rule, both of which we think provide good reasons for consultation. But what about everybody else? Why take part in what you have every reason to expect will be a meaningless—but time-consuming and blood pressure-raising—exercise?

To you "consulting parties," as the ACHP regulations call you, we can only say that consultation is the only game in town, other than litigation. And if you try to litigate without first exhausting all the available "administrative remedies," your case is likely to get thrown out of court before you get started. Consultation—whether it's for real consultation or just a flim-flam—is one of the major administrative remedies the law provides, so you pretty much have to take part if you want to have any influence over the outcome. If you don't, you're essentially giving up without trying. And sometimes, despite the best/worst efforts of those in charge of the process, consultation *does* accomplish things.

In deciding whether to consult, you—especially you non-sponsor, not-agency consulting parties—need to think about what dispute resolution specialists call your BATNA—"best alternative to a negotiated agreement." In other words, what can you get if you *don't* consult? Maybe you have a way to impose your will on the sponsor or government agency, perhaps based on a treaty or some other legal instrument giving you special power. Most often, though, your BATNA is likely to be pretty thin, and if you want to get anything at all out of the situation, you'd better come to the table. But keep the BATNA in mind, because it may change as the consultation proceeds, and in some cases it may improve to the point at which walking away, just saying no, becomes the most rational thing to do.

So How Should We Consult?

Applying the Golden Rule, how would *you* like to be consulted? We don't know about you, but *we* would like to be consulted in approximately the following manner:

1. Initiate consultation early, before the key decisions have been made, the investments assembled, the permits applied for. Don't wait till you've made up your mind, selected your site, developed your design, set your heart and your pocketbook on a particular way of achieving your objectives.

2. Go into consultation with an attitude that gives us a fighting chance for our arguments to prevail. Don't go into it with your mind utterly made up and your ears deaf to our concerns. Be willing to consider what we say and what we propose.

3. Explain to us, in words we can understand, what it is you're thinking of doing. Provide us with a full description of what you propose, with maps and plans that actually represent the proposal in ways we can understand, and information on what you think both the impacts and the benefits of your project will be. Do this *before* you've decided to undertake the project, or invested too much time and money in establishing how and where to do it. Provide us with updated information as the consultation proceeds. And don't try to shift the information-gathering burden to us; don't try to demand that we explain the environment or the impacts to you. After all, it's your project, not ours.

4. But show respect for what we *do* tell you; don't dismiss our concerns about birds because we're not ornithologists, about scenery because you don't find the place very scenic, about spirits in the landscape because you don't believe in them.

5. Communicate with us, in back and forth dialogue, about:
    a. Why you *want* to do what you want to do;
    b. What its purpose is and why that purpose is desirable;
    c. Alternative ways of achieving the project's purposes—including those you think of, those we think of, and those that others may bring up;
    d. Any problems we may have with what you want to do;

    e.   Ways to resolve our problems; and

    f.   If you don't think you can resolve our problems, why you think that.

6.   Really try to reach agreement with us about how our problems will be resolved, and if we do agree, commit that agreement to writing.

7.   Do what you've agreed to do, or

8.   If we can't reach agreement, document how and why we've tried to do so, and do whatever you *can* do to address our problems.

That, we think, is consultation in a nutshell, and that admittedly very simple formulation informs the rest of this book.

But If You Really Don't Want To...

If you're working for the project sponsor or an overseeing agency, you may not want to consult. You may be quite sure that what you, your agency, your company or your client are planning is the right and necessary thing to do, and you really don't care what anyone else thinks. You may feel that you have your marching orders, and that's that. You may want to interpret the laws and regulations that require or encourage consultation as narrowly as possible, so as to consult as little as possible, with as few people as possible, about as few issues as possible. Or you may personally be perfectly happy to consult, but believe that you can't do it and keep your job, or advance in your organization.

If that's where you stand, then you can read this book but do the opposite of everything we recommend. You'll probably get along fine, though we hope you don't.

CHAPTER 3

Seeking

Consultation means the process of seeking... the views of other participants...
(36 CFR § 800.16(F))

Seeking the views—the interests, concerns, hopes, fears, and, importantly, the ideas—of others is something that needs to happen throughout any consultation, and it needs to involve everyone who's interested. Primarily, though, it's the project sponsor and the oversight agency (if any) who are responsible for seeking people's views. It's they, after all, who are (or at least should be) invested in bringing consultation to a mutually agreeable conclusion.

Seeking views of course means asking for them, but it also involves being open to expressions of concern, and alert to the possibility that someone has a concern but is for some reason unable or unwilling to express it. If they're not recognized and dealt with, such concerns can blow up into real problems. And of course, new concerns can come up at any time.

But seeking views is also the logical first step in consultation—once you've determined who you need to consult. Let's consider ways to do it.

Identifying and Engaging Consulting Parties

How do you determine who to consult? Some consulting parties may be prescribed by law. If you're working under Section 106 of NHPA, the State and/or Tribal Historic Preservation Officer(s) (SHPOs, THPOs) *must* be consulted, but they're not the only ones. You also must consult with poten-

Claudia Nissley and Thomas F. King, "Seeking" in *Consultation and Cultural Heritage: Let Us Reason Together,* pp. 28-57. © 2014 Left Coast Press, Inc. All rights reserved.

tially affected Indian tribes (whether or not they have THPOs) and with local governments. Finally, at various points the regulations either identify other parties with "interests" as "entitled" to participate, or simply permit them to do so, leaving it up to the sponsor or oversight agency to find them (or not). The interests of such parties may be economic (the potential to gain or lose money if the project does or does not go forward). They may be jurisdictional—say, the interests of a regional planning body. They may be cultural, historic, or aesthetic, including but certainly not limited to interests in recorded or not-yet recorded historic places, or in the area's history or environment, or in how the area looks or sounds or smells.

If you're consulting under the Endangered Species Act you're required to consult a much narrower range of parties—essentially only the U.S. Fish and Wildlife Service or the National Marine Fisheries Service, and perhaps state and tribal fish and wildlife agencies. NEPA's consultation requirements are similarly focused on official, governmental, and ostensibly expert entities. But the fact that you may be *required* to consult with only a limited range of entities doesn't mean that it's smart or responsible to stay within those limits. Remember the two dead good reasons for consultation—you're looking for things you don't know or haven't thought about, and you're trying to encourage people to accept, or at least not violently oppose, what you're trying to do. You're trying to avoid surprises. The more broadly you consult, the more likely you are to find out what you need to know but don't already know, and you're certainly not going to build agreement if you don't talk with people. So, though you may be able to *get away with* consulting only a few entities with, in the words of the NEPA regulations, "jurisdiction by law or special expertise" (40 CFR § 14-2.19(a)), our strong recommendation is to go beyond what you can get away with. *Consult with everybody who may be concerned.*

Rio Tinto, a multi-national mining and minerals company, says that to find and address impacts on the cultural environment:

> Consultation should include the full range of stakeholders involved in an area's cultural heritage including, but not limited to: historical or traditional users and owners of the cultural heritage, local communities, indigenous and minority peoples, descendent families, government agencies, religious institutions, national and local

museums and cultural institutes, the scientific community, local historical groups and non-governmental organizations (Rio Tinto 2011:25).

How do you determine who all those people are? You ask around. Ask the parties with whom you're required to consult who else they recommend. When you contact these other parties, ask them about others, too. Ask other agencies, companies, consultants, academics, organizations. Check media archives for information on previous projects in the area; who was concerned about those? Find out who was involved and try to contact them.

If your project is a small, simple one with little potential for conflict with other people's interests, there may be very few people or groups to consult, and you may not have to put out much effort to find them. If it's a bigger or more controversial project, though, there may be a lot of interested parties, and you may not find them all at the outset. That's OK; consultation ought to be a fluid, organic, iterative process, and consulting parties can be added at any time. Conversely, some parties may drop out for one reason or another as consultation goes forward, and that's OK too.

The organic character of consultation is something that's lost on a lot of people, particularly those who consult only because they're required to. If you're undertaking consultation just to be able to say you've done it, to check the "consultation" box on the check-list, you're likely to want things to be cut and dried. "We'll contact the people on a list we've gotten somewhere, and if you're not on the list, or don't contact *us* within X number of days, or send the right kind of letter or email to the right place, you're out of luck; you've missed your chance."

This is something to be alert to if you're *not* the proponent or sponsor and want to consult. Don't wait for a sponsor or agency official to contact you. If you hear about a project and are interested in consulting, try to find out who the responsible parties are and contact them, preferably in writing so there's a record that you did. Then try to meet agency-imposed deadlines even if they're grossly unreasonable (but you can object loudly while doing so). If you miss a deadline, you may need to remind the responsible agency—forcefully, perhaps—that as a citizen and taxpayer you have consultative rights that are not absolutely constrained by arbitrary rules and deadlines.

Unless, of course, they *are*. Some agencies have highly structured rules governing how a member of the public can "intervene" in a case. These may actually impose hard and fast deadlines, and specify in some detail the form and content of official filings that must be followed in order to get to the consultation table, or at least to get there and be paid attention to. If you're dealing with that kind of agency, you're probably going to have no choice but to play by their rules, and it's important to learn them, whatever they are.

Still, though, it's the responsibility of the oversight agency and/or project sponsor to seek the views of consulting parties, and ideally that shouldn't be a one-shot deal. Consultation should involve a constant reaching out and welcoming in, because good ideas can come from anywhere, anytime, and there are lots of good reasons for missing deadlines. It's both foolish and unjust to keep someone away from the consulting table just because they missed a deadline.

Building Relationships

If you're in a position to build and maintain relationships with those you may need to consult—if, for example, you work for an agency that administers a particular piece of land over the course of many years—you're well advised to try to identify potential consulting parties and develop relationships of trust and respect with them *before* you have a particular project for them to consider. In Innes/Booher (2010) terms, you probably *are* more or less interdependent with your neighbors, and exploring ways to collaborate may be in your agency's best interest as well as theirs. So hold open houses, take part in community events, sponsor a "friends" group for your park, national forest, or military base. Ask people for their views about how to manage your facility in general, and pay attention to them. Get to know the leaders of your local Indian tribe, Native Hawaiian community, neighborhood, or town—and its non-leaders, who may be leaders next year. This will give you some of the information you need to identify consulting parties when the time comes to deal with a particular project, and it will make you a known quantity to your potential consulting partners, rather than a mysterious stranger, here today and gone tomorrow. Of course, if you're working on a specific project like a road, a bridge, or a pipeline, so that you really *are* here today and gone tomorrow, this option isn't open to you.

Relationship-building ought to be a two-way street. If you're a long-term resident or user of an area's lands and resources, it will behoove you, too, to try to get together with the agencies responsible for managing them, and with those who are likely to oversee projects in the area, well before you have an actual project to deal with. Getting to know the forest supervisor or park superintendent or district ranger or resident engineer will make it a lot more likely that you'll get the word when a project is being planned, and that you'll find sympathetic ears and voices around the consultation table when you get there.

Yes, this "seeking" is beginning to seem like a lot of work, and it's not usually very explicitly required by law, but just doing the minimum that's legally required is likely to get a sponsor or oversight agency in trouble—not every time, but often enough that it's worth considering doing more. And if you're not the sponsor or agency, you need to work every possible angle to make yourself known, and to build your credibility. However unfair it may be, the cards are stacked against you, and you've got to do whatever you can to even the odds.

The Risks in Relying on Authorities

There's naturally a temptation—especially if you're in an official position yourself—to consult only with government officials or others in authority, or only with those who are recommended by someone in authority. After all, they're in authority, so surely they're authoritative, right?

Wrong. Authority doesn't mean omniscience. Plus, a lot of people who are assigned authority by law aren't given the financial or organizational resources to exercise that authority very well. Environmental, cultural heritage and historic preservation authorities in governments everywhere are congenitally under-funded and overworked. Their inevitable adaptations to this condition—hiring lightly qualified staff, setting up standard procedures that can be followed without a lot of thinking—do not enhance the reliability of their advice.

In late 2012, as we were starting work on this book, the case of Amity Pueblo was in the news (e.g., Alonzo 2012). This ancient village site in Arizona included the ruins of a multi-room pueblo—visible on the surface of the ground, recorded by archaeologists, and regularly visited by spiritual practitioners from Zuni and other pueblos. The Arizona State Game and Fish Department wanted to put in a public fishing pond, and got money from the U.S. Fish and Wildlife Service to do so—right next to the pueblo. Project planners contacted the State Historic Preservation Officer under NHPA Section 106, saying that the project, they thought, would not affect any historic places. This was an utterly absurd assumption, but the SHPO—who probably was able to devote fifteen minutes to reviewing the documentation at a desk in Phoenix—agreed. The Game and Fish Department took that as an OK to proceed, and the project went forward. Nobody consulted the people of Zuni pueblo and other communities with ancestral ties to Amity, and before long the bulldozers were churning up human bones and artifacts. The project was stopped—at not-yet calculated cost to the taxpayers—but not before at least ten graves had been destroyed and a good deal of the site torn up. The people of Zuni and other pueblo communities were understandably outraged, and at this writing the various government officials are busily pointing fingers at one another. The U.S. Fish and Wildlife Service, whose funds supported the project, has held meetings with tribal and state officials in an effort to determine how to proceed, but as far as we know nothing has been agreed to.

If someone had talked to the people of Zuni, it's very unlikely that the destruction would have occurred. The pond might not have gotten built, at least in Game and Fish's preferred location, but it now looks like that's not going to happen anyway, and the decision not to build it could have been made at much lower cost, with much less emotional stress for all concerned. And of course, it could have been made without destroying graves and a place of great cultural importance to the Zuni and others. The "authority" in this case—the SHPO—*could* have been the one to talk to Zuni, but it wasn't really the SHPO's responsibility, and they were probably the least equipped to do it in terms of time, money, and first-hand knowledge. They could have—should have—told the Game and Fish Department or the Fish and Wildlife Service to talk to the Zuni; we don't know why they didn't. But the fact that they didn't doesn't relieve the proponent agencies of their consultative responsibilities, or their responsibility to avoid bulldozing graves.

So, ask the authorities, sure, but don't assume that they have mystic powers or crystal balls that enable them to know all and see all. Ask others, and use your own eyes and brain. "We're proposing to dig this big hole in the ground right next to an ancient pueblo; maybe we ought to talk with some pueblo people."

When to Start

It's too late to be early.—Tribal representative at a delayed "informational" meeting on a 2011 project

When should you initiate consultation? The simple answer is "as early as possible," and that's the right answer, too. The earlier you get started, the more flexibility everyone has to deal with whatever issues come up; the later you start, the more likely it is that people will have gotten into intractable positions. And generally speaking, people want to be consulted when their opinions can actually influence decision-making and outcomes.

But "start early" is a little *too* simple, because you need to know enough about the project under review to tell the potential consulting parties about it, or what you think of it, and you need to be able to share enough information to let everyone understand the situation and come to reasonable conclusions. This creates a certain inevitable chicken-egg situation. Which comes first, the information or the consultation? The less than satisfying answer is "neither" and "both." Consultation often has to begin based on very limited, conceptual information, and gain specificity as information is developed. Consultation should both benefit from and guide information gathering.

In recent years there's been a lot of interest among environmental impact assessment (EIA) practitioners in "Strategic Environmental Assessment" (SEA—see SEA Info.Net n.d.) and "Programmatic Environmental Impact Statements" (PEIS). Among historic preservation agencies in the U.S., "Programmatic Agreements" (PAs) are similarly popular (c.f. King 2013:190-98). The idea is to back up and look at big pictures—whole government programs, plans, and policies, or big regions, in lieu of examining or dealing with the impacts of particular projects. This makes a lot of sense, but not necessarily when it comes to consultation. Agencies have trouble engaging the public in consultation on SEA and PAs—if they even try. The reason, of course, is that at the level that SEA, PEISs and PAs are done, everything is abstract; nothing is hitting members of the public where they live, immediately threatening their easily perceived environments. It's a lot easier to understand that building a new highway between Upper Downtown and Middle Edgerton may have impacts on your environment (especially if you live between the two places) than it is to grasp the likely impacts of transportation planning policy in southwest East Dakota.

Even if you're not operating at the ethereal levels represented by SEA, PEISs and PAs—even if you're planning a fishing hole in Arizona—you have somehow to balance the need for early consultation with the need to share information that's specific enough to allow people to relate to it. This doesn't mean that you ought to design your fishing hole, get rights to use the land, and buy gas for the bulldozers before you start consulting, but it does mean that you ought to be able to show on a map where you're thinking of putting in the pond (preferably, several alternative locations where you might put it) and say something about why you want to build it and what variables influence your choice of sites.

Remember the Golden Rule: if somebody were asking you to consult about something, what information would you want them to be able to share with you? That's what you ought to supply to your potential consulting parties—but you ought to do it as early as you possibly can. No matter what, you ought to consult early enough that the results can influence your, or your agency's, or your client's decisions. That's the core requirement of most relevant laws; there's no point in consultation if it can have no influence on decision-making.

If you're consulting on behalf of a potentially affected party, try to understand the box the agency or sponsor may find itself in, trying to consult early but at the same time to muster the information everyone needs. Don't expect them to come in with fully developed project plans if they're trying to consult you early. They shouldn't *have* fully developed plans; developing such plans should be informed by consultation. If you demand too much information, in too much detail, there will be little for the agency or sponsor to do but put off consultation until it can develop the data—which will cost money and take time. This in turn may make them become invested in precisely the kind of project you don't want to see.

Public Notices

We're often asked if our clients—when our clients are agencies—need to publish public notices to attract consulting parties. Sometimes we're even asked if publishing a public notice constitutes consultation (answer: No!).

A typical public notice, published in local media and often posted on the worldwide web, says something like:

> The East Dakota Bureau of Fish and Flowers (EDBFF), with funding from the U.S. Department of Flowers and Fish (DFF), proposes to construct a fishpond in the SE quarter of the NW quarter of Section 27, Township 45 North Range 18 West, near the town of Townley. This public notice is issued as part of DFF's responsibilities under 36 CFR Part 800, the regulations which implement Section 106 of the National Historic Preservation Act (NHPA) of 1966, as amended, 16 USC § 470. The Section 106 regulations require DFF to seek ways to avoid, minimize, or mitigate any adverse effects of this project, and to consider the views of the public on preservation issues. In this public notice, DFF is providing information about the proposed fishpond and its effects on historic properties. We are also seeking public input on the project, and would appreciate comments identifying any concerns or issues pertinent to the project by February 30, 2015.

The notice goes on, usually, to provide a map and a brief description of the project, and to specify where comments should be sent.

There's nothing wrong with publishing public notices, and some laws and regulations require them, but you should not rely on them to bring consulting parties flocking to the table. Even if everyone who might want to consult is a native reader of English and subscribes to the local paper, few may read public notices (usually published along with other legal notices, deeply buried in the back pages in fine print). And those who do decide to read your notice may have trouble working their way through the bureaucratic language. If someone is not a native speaker and reader of English, the chances of their catching the notice and responding to it are almost nil.

Bottom line: publishing a notice may be required by law, and it may bring in some people who ought to be consulted, but don't count on it.

Some agencies and project proponents (and their lawyers) *do* rely on public notices, however, so if you're a concerned member of the public you may need to train yourself to pay attention to the media in which such things are published in your area—often the "legal notices" section of a local newspaper. Since notices tend to follow standard formats, it may be hard to distinguish those projects that concern you from those that don't. We don't have an answer to this, other than just to read a number of notices and get used to how they're organized, so you can whip through the chaff and get to what's interesting to you. Many agencies now post their notices on the worldwide web, which may make it either easier or harder to keep track of them, depending on how web-savvy you are.

Public Hearings

What about public hearings, then? Are public hearings a good way to contact consulting parties?

The public hearing is a mainstay of American democracy; everybody holds public hearings. You get a facility—maybe the City Council's chambers, maybe the high school gymnasium, whatever you think will seat everybody who's likely to attend—and you publish notice that you're holding a hearing on whatever the project is. The notice for a public hearing typically looks something like this what is shown on the next page.

By and large, Americans love public hearings, and citizens' groups tend to get very upset if they're not held as part of decision making about significant projects. But public hearings are *not consultation*. They *may* be one method of seeking the views of concerned people, but they may also obscure such views and contribute to their being ignored. They often frustrate the purposes of consultation. As a matter of fact, they tend to frustrate their *own* purposes. As the planning scholars Judith Innes and David Booher succinctly commented in a 2004 critique, "public hearings…do not work" (Innes & Booher 2004:419).

For one thing, they often don't elicit much in the way of thoughtful comment. Since speakers are always limited in the time they can speak, and since there's almost never any dialogue that might clarify people's concerns, what you wind up with is a sort of crude statistic: X percent of people like the

EAST DAKOTA BUREAU OF FISH AND FLOWERS

NOTICE OF PUBLIC HEARING

SUBJECT: Proposed Fish Pond near Town of Townley

PURPOSE: The purpose of this hearing is to inform the public about the proposed project, and to elicit information and concerns from the public relating to impacts on cultural resources.

Tuesday, February 30, 2015, 11:00 a.m.

Auditorium, Townley High School, 823 Grand Ave.,

Townley, East Dakota

ORAL TESTIMONY WILL BE BY INVITATION ONLY

Persons wishing to present pertinent testimony to the Bureau at the above hearing should complete and return the enclosed reply form as soon as possible. It is important that the reply form be fully completed and returned so that persons may be notified in the event of emergency postponement or cancellation.

Oral testimony will be limited to 10 minutes' duration. In preparing the order of witnesses, the Bureau will attempt to accommodate individual requests to speak at particular times in view of special circumstances. These requests should be made on the attached reply form or communicated to Bureau staff as early as possible.

Twenty copies of any prepared testimony should be submitted at the hearing registration desk. The Bureau would appreciate advance receipt of prepared statements.

project; Y percent don't. X percent are concerned about N factor; Y percent are interested in Z. Those sorts of data may be of some value, but they often just generate fog.

For another thing, public hearings can be frustrating and irritating; they tend to be highly structured, requiring people to sit through lengthy presentations about the project and its benefits and then to squeeze their own comments into short sound bites. They often don't reveal very much about anything, and they aren't even aimed at resolving anyone's problems. Project proponents speak glowingly of their projects and say as little as possible about their possible defects. Much of what's said is meaningless rhetoric.

This has two typical results. Some people just tune out, either not attending at all or more or less going to sleep in their chairs. Most of those responsible for holding the hearing—the agency representatives, their consultants, maybe local cooperating agencies, representatives of the project proponent—usually tune out too; they can't avoid attending, but they can sit up on stage with poker faces and turn their minds to their plans for the weekend. Other people—members of the public—get mad and may more or less act out their anger, berating the project proponents or the overseeing agencies, expounding on what terrible effects the project will have, harking back to previous injustices and destruction, and generally ratcheting up the level of conflict. All this wastes time and often *impedes* sensible consultation (See Innes & Booher 2004 for further discussion).

There are lots of alternatives to public hearings, which may be more effective for eliciting concerns and less likely to create or exacerbate conflict. The New Jersey Department of Environmental Protection long ago published a thoughtful workbook on the subject (Pflugh & Shannon 1991), suggesting things like open houses and structured information exchanges, coffee klatches, focus groups, and interactive briefings. Simply holding smaller, more informal meetings may work better than staging large, formal public hearings. Spacing meetings out over a period of time may help, or conducting them in different locations or with different interest groups. This may itself complicate consultation, however, if it comes to be suspected that different groups are hearing different things, or that "deals" are being hatched in secret. It may be possible to defuse these suspicious simply by being open about the fact that multiple meetings *are* being held, explaining why they're being held, and posting information about each meeting and its outcomes on websites for all to review.

Ineffective and pointless as they can be, public hearings have a lot of fans, and they do have the advantage of giving everyone who attends a uniform body of information and some kind of opportunity to be heard. Like public notice, one or more public hearings may be necessary, but they're merely one—not very good—way to convey and receive information; they are not a substitute for real dialogue. They should make some segments of the population (those who read notices and relate well to public events) aware of your project, so they may be helpful in identifying consulting parties, but their very nature may generate hostilities that might not exist otherwise.

Bottom line: Hold public hearings if they're required by law, if people really want them, or if there seems to be some other good reason to have them, but don't opt for them automatically. Explore alternatives that meet whatever legal requirements exist, and don't *ever* think of a public hearing as, or as an alternative to, consultation.

If you're among those a hearing is supposed to hear—or a notice is supposed to notify—never, never accept the notice or hearing as the be-all and end-all of consultation. Read the notice and respond to it clearly and concisely; attend the hearing and be heard, but don't stop there. Insist that the agency or proponent pay attention to the results of the notice and/or hearing, and that it go on to consult. Tell them that you want to consult; tell them why, and insist that they respond. If they're not responsive, or put you off, see what bigger guns you can bring to bear—your congressional delegation, local government officials, organizations with name recognition.

Respecting Cultural Differences

The need to respect cultural differences is pretty widely accepted in government and industry today, but acceptance in principle does not automatically translate into practice. Many commonly used systems for eliciting public concerns about projects were established in law and practice before there was widespread appreciation of the fact that different cultural groups have different ways of interacting with others and particularly with people in authority. Most such systems reflect the traditions of the European Enlightenment—which is all fine, but not everyone is a product of those traditions. And those traditions themselves—notably the principle that government requires the knowledgeable consent or at least acquiescence of the governed—demand that other traditions be respectfully considered when we ask people to participate in planning.

In his 1976 book *Beyond Culture,* Edward T. Hall showed how the communication styles of different cultural groups can be arrayed along a continuum from "low context" to "high context." Low-context people communicate mostly to share information, focusing on the specific subject at hand and shutting out other considerations. A low-context communicator sticks to the "facts of the matter"—*this* project, *these* impacts, the situation on the ground and the participants in consultation at *this* time. Higher context societies communicate in ways that may reflect a number of social contexts besides that of transferring data from one person to another about a specific subject, or resolving a specific shared problem. A person from a high-context society is likely to be concerned at least as much about status relationships and social expectations as about the "objective facts" and "real world solutions" valued by a low-context individual. He or she is likely to conceive of this project, these impacts, this time, these participants in terms of historical and social relationships, how this project, these impacts, or these interactions are like (or unlike) others in the past, or how they fit into broad patterns of interaction, status, and power.

Raymond Cohen (1997) showed how communication breakdowns between negotiators from high-context and low-context societies have been costly and even fatal in international diplomacy. The same danger exists in consultation about environmental and cultural resource issues, particularly but not exclusively where indigenous communities are or ought to be among the consulting parties.

When we're at the stage of seeking people's views and trying to elicit their concerns, we need to think about the cultural contexts in which those views and concerns may need to be expressed, and what barriers may exist to their expression. For instance, in indigenous societies (among others), a great deal of knowledge about environmental, historical, and cultural matters may be held by elders, or by subgroups with societal charters to manage it (for example, particular clans, medicine people or societies, spiritual practitioners). Members of these subgroups may be deeply constrained in how freely they can share information and with whom they can share it. Just waltzing into such a high-context society and asking its elders to spill the beans about what's important to them in the environment, for example, is probably going to yield bad results. Not only will it fail to produce the desired information; it may close down consultation before it even begins. Trying to tap into "traditional ecological knowledge," often reduced to the acronym "TEK," is popular among some environmental analysts (c.f. Menzies 2006). This can be very positive both in terms of understanding environmental processes and addressing local interests, but to use TEK, one has to respect the tradition-saturated cultures and minds in which such knowledge resides.

A well-known if now rather hoary example of what failing to consider cultural differences can do is the 1995 New Mexico case that came to be inscribed in law as *Pueblo of Sandia v. United States*. In this case the U.S. Forest Service, conducting EIA and NHPA Section 106 review of plans for road and facility improvements in a canyon on the Cibola National Forest,

> ...mailed [letters] to local Indian tribes, including the Sandia Pueblo, and individual tribal members who were known to be familiar with traditional cultural properties. The letters requested detailed information describing the location of ... [cultural] sites, activities conducted there, and the frequency of the activities. They also asked tribes to provide maps of the sites, drawn at a scale of 1:24,000 or better, as well as documentation of the historic nature of the property.[1]

As the court later told the Forest Service in no uncertain terms, the Service should have understood—based both on readily available government-wide guidance and on ethnographic data—that there was no way in the world the tribes would provide that kind of information. The canyon was actually an area of considerable spiritual significance to Sandia Pueblo people, and information about it is regarded by them as having power that can't be dealt with lightly. Sandia Pueblo, in short, is a high-context society in which social, cultural, and spiritual beliefs trump sharing "objective" data with government authorities.

So the tribes didn't provide the requested data, and the Forest Service went ahead with its plans, until Sandia Pueblo filed suit and eventually brought the project to a screeching halt. The Court of Appeals found that the Forest Service had not made the "reasonable and good faith effort" to identify historic properties that is required by the NHPA Section 106 regulations—because, in essence, it hadn't done a reasonable job of identifying and communicating with likely consulting parties.

In a more recent case, *Comanche Nation v. United States*, the U.S. District Court for the Western District of Oklahoma,[2] in effectively halting a

U.S. Army construction project in Oklahoma, made a similar finding about the Army's failure to communicate intelligently with the Comanche Nation, commenting that

> It has been said that the NHPA requires an agency to "stop, look and listen;" the evidence in the present case suggests that Defendants merely paused, glanced, and turned a deaf ear to warnings of adverse impact. Thus, Defendants' efforts fell short of the reasonable and good faith efforts required by the law.

In late 2010, in *Quechan Tribe of the Fort Yuma Reservation v. U.S. Department of the Interior*,[3] the District Court for the Southern District of California awarded a preliminary injunction to the Quechan Tribe, setting aside a U.S. government permit for the development of a solar energy project on government land.[4] Here again the main flaw found by the court in the government's permitting process was its failure to consult meaningfully. Reviewing the extensive government filings purporting to show that consultation had occurred, the court noted that

> First, the sheer volume of documents is not meaningful. The number of letters, reports, meetings, etc. and the size of the various documents doesn't in itself show [that]…consultation occurred.

> Second, [the government's] communications are replete with recitals of law…, professions of good intent, and solicitations to consult with the Tribe. But mere *pro forma* recitals do not, by themselves, show [that the government] actually complied with the law.

> [The government's] invitation to "consult"… amounted to little more than a general request for the Tribe to gather its own information…and disclose it at public meetings. Because of the lack of information, it was impossible for the Tribe to have consulted meaningfully as required in applicable regulations.

> The Tribe's consulting rights should have been respected. It is clear that did not happen here.

We suspect that in all three of these cases, the agencies were treating the consultative requirements of NHPA Section 106—and probably the entire EIA process—as procedural formalities to be gotten out of the way as quickly and cheaply as possible. They probably didn't much care what the tribes said, as long as they could check off the box on a checklist saying they'd asked them about cultural concerns. But even if they did not make this fundamental error, they erred by assuming that indigenous groups would handle a request for information in the way that, say, a city government probably would—"You want that information to plan your project? OK, here it is." It just doesn't necessarily work that way—not with tribes, not with other indigenous groups, not with any high-context community.

How *does* it work? How can you elicit necessary information across cultural boundaries, in a respectful manner?

First, of course, simply by *recognizing that you have, or may have, cultural boundaries to work across*. Are there indigenous groups that may be affected or involved? Other groups that may not relate easily to standard ways of eliciting information and concerns? Review background data, and again, ask around. Others who have worked in the area, maybe planned projects in the area, may be able to advise you, as may local planners, academics, and citizens' organizations. Keep in mind, though, that all these people may have their own axes to grind, and may direct you mostly toward others who share their points of view.

Second, by *giving yourself the time* to find out about and interact with the community. Don't assume you can just send them a letter or get them to fill out a questionnaire—unless, of course, this turns out to be what the community is used to, and thinks is OK.

Try to learn something about how the community relates to outsiders, and how its people respond to inquiries. Find out something about its history, its internal institutions and organizations, its common ways of interacting with outsiders. This may require some serious research, or it may require just asking around, reviewing some web sites. Understanding how things—especially interactive things—are done locally will help you tailor your approach to consultation so as to gain people's respect, and to avoid turning them off.

Review your own assumptions. In the *Pueblo of Sandia* case, the Forest Service must have assumed that it needed to know the locations of specific cultural sites, the activities tribal people carried out there, and how often they carried them out. They must have thought they needed maps, and all the other documentation they asked for. But did they? Maybe somewhere down the line, but certainly not at the very outset, when they were (or should have been) just trying to undertake consultation. And maybe not at all. Which leads to another rule:

Don't ask for more than you need. The Forest Service really needed to ask Sandia Pueblo and the other tribes only three things:

1. Do you have any concerns about what we might do in the canyon?

2. If so, would you like to consult with us about your concerns and how we can resolve them?

3. If so, how would you like to consult? When, where, in what sort of format or according to what plan and schedule?

The same three questions, asked early and respectfully, would have gotten consultation off on a good footing in the Oklahoma and California cases. They very probably would have elicited helpful and cooperative responses.

This is not to say that the response would have been "sure, fine, no problem." Sandia Pueblo people saw the canyon (not just specific spots in it) as culturally sensitive, spiritually powerful, and they wanted the Forest Service to respect these perceptions. The Comanche were concerned about the Army's new construction blocking the view of a rocky hill to which and from which they offer prayers. The Quechan didn't appreciate solar arrays being flung up all over a landscape that they viewed as a spiritual place and that contained the buried remains of their ancestors. These were real issues that would have had to be addressed. We can't know now how they might have been addressed, or how addressing them would have influenced government decision making, but if nothing else, respectful consultation, taking cultural differences into account, would have placed the government in all three cases on more solid legal ground.

Take Off Your Specialist Hat

Whether you're an archaeologist, a historian, an environmental scientist, or an engineer, you've been trained to think and interact and report information in particular ways, which have probably come to fit you like a pair of old shoes. Others don't think and interact in the same ways, so *don't assume that they do.* The minimum information you actually need is *not* necessarily what you'd automatically look for or provide in an archaeological survey report or an engineering plan; it's the minimum you need to initiate consultation or reveal that nobody feels the need to consult. And that probably means answers only to those three questions: do you have a concern; if so, do you want to consult about it; and if so, how?

We don't know for sure, but we suspect that whoever drafted the Forest Service's letter in the Sandia Pueblo case was an archaeologist, and archaeologists were key players in the Comanche and Quechan cases. The questions asked in the Forest Service's letter are the kinds of questions an archaeologist quite naturally expects to ask and answer about "archaeological sites"—what are they, where are they on the map, what are their boundaries, why are they important? The drafter just assumed (we assume) that the tribes would find such questions relevant and sensible, and so would be willing to answer them. In the Comanche case, once an archaeological survey had "cleared" the project site, the Army assumed its cultural worries were over. In the California case, the government relied on archaeological survey to guide the placement of solar panels. We don't mean to pick on archaeology—we were both trained in that field—but in all three cases—and many others[5]—agencies and project proponents have been and continue to be misled by the assumptions and worldviews of a particular academic discipline. The discipline may be archaeology, architectural history, environmental science, engineering, biology, or any of a number of other fields, none of which routinely train practitioners to deal with living people and their environmental concerns, especially across cultural boundaries. Many practitioners pick up people skills on the job, and do fine, but those skills are what an agency or project proponent should look for, rather than assuming that because Tess Trowel is an archaeologist she must be good at interacting with Indians. And Tess, of course, ought to try to be aware of her own limitations, and either seek to get past them or not volunteer for or accept an assignment to do work that's beyond her competence.

Don't Ask Them to Do Your Job

Another flaw in the government's approach in all three of the cases outlined above was that it expected the tribes to do its work for it. The Forest Service in the Sandia case was the most blunt: go out and buy those maps, tribes; mark them up, compose an essay on what makes the sites significant, and we government authorities in our wisdom will consider whether to believe and respect what you tell us. Pretty autocratic. Similarly, the Army in Oklahoma expected the Comanche to pipe up if they had any problem with the project—if they could figure out the draft environmental documents in which it was described—within a tight deadline. And in the California case the government wanted the Tribe "to gather its own information…and disclose it at public meetings" (see above).

It's not the job of a community or an SHPO—or anybody else—to describe the environment someone's project will affect. It's the job of the responsible agency, or the project sponsor with the agency's oversight. If you're the agency official or the sponsor's representative, it's *your* job. Sure, the community or tribe or SHPO probably knows more about it than you do; they probably can put their hands on relevant data more readily than you can, and—at least in the case of a tribe or other community—they're the ones who are concerned about the place and how you'll affect it. That knowledge and those concerns ought to incline them to consult with you, but there's no reason they should invest time and money in collecting, organizing, and presenting data to you. You can certainly ask them for information, but recognize that they're doing you a favor if they supply it. And again, think about what information you really need, and let that be the limit on what you seek. Having precise dots or squares or squiggles on a map and clear narratives about a place's significance may seem necessary to you as an engineer, as a historian, or just as a tidy person, but do you really need that level of detail? If you don't, don't try to get the community to provide it. If you *do* really need it, think about how to get it without burdening the consulting parties.

If you represent the affected community, or some part of it, don't let the sponsor or agency get away with shifting the information-gathering burden to you, but at the same time try to think strategically about what information it's useful to supply, and how. For example, when asked to consult about the impacts of a proposed zinc mine on cultural places, the Mole Lake Sokaogon Ojibwe community in Wisconsin politely declined to cooperate with the sponsor's "cultural resources" studies, which it didn't trust. Instead it had its own study done, characterizing the value of the landscape in terms that were accurate from the community's point of view but understandable to federal regulators (Nesper, Willow & King 2002). This effort cost the community some money, but was helpful as part of a strategy that in the end defeated the proposal and brought the landscape under Ojibwe control.

Consider Differences in Capabilities, Knowledge, and Interests

Even if you're not consulting across obvious cultural boundaries, members of the community with which you're dealing are likely to view the world, and understand it, and operate in it, in ways that are different from the way you do. And if you're representing an agency or sponsor, members of the community are likely to have priorities and experience constraints that are very different from those of your employer or client.

For one thing, they probably have to work for a living at jobs that do not relate in any way to the proposed project. Certainly you have to work for a living too, but your job is, we assume, either to promote your (or your client's) project or to review its impacts on the environment. In simple terms, you get paid to take part in consultation; most of them don't. Many of them *do* get paid to do other things—teach school, tend bar, run a farm, drive a truck; they need to do these things to keep themselves and their families alive, and their jobs have schedules attached. You need to think about this, and ask about it, when setting up your consultation plans. When and where is it convenient for them to get together, or would they prefer *not* to get together but to communicate by letter, email, or phone? Try to find ways to make consultation work for them.

They also *may not have a lot of money*, either as individuals or as members of a group. It may be hard for them to drive in from the country and afford a hotel room in the city, or to pay for meals and gas. Nobody's paying them per diem. Think about how to make consultation affordable for them.

Then there's the matter of *language*. Even if they're not technically from different cultures, they may not speak English as their native language, and even if they do, they almost certainly do not speak bureaucratese or the jargon of the various technical specialties involved in impact assessment, cultural resource management, and planning. Try to adjust your own language—not to dumb it down, but to make it understandable to people outside your own cluster of cubicles or your academic department.

And their *cultural, social, and political values* may differ from yours, perhaps to such an extent that if you wear your own values too brilliantly emblazoned on your sleeve, you'll cut off communication. We're not suggesting that you abandon your own principles, but you may not need to advertise them too obviously, and you absolutely should not assume that others share them. You may think that Conservatives or Liberals or Libertarians or Fundamentalist Atheists are ignorant nutcases, but if you're going to be consulting with people of that persuasion, it's unwise to push your point of view. You're not trying to change their politics or beliefs; you're trying to address their concerns about the project that's under review.

Their *interests and concerns* may not fit readily into the pigeonholes in which you and your organization are used to putting things. We recently reviewed a report that evaluated a collection of structures and sites as to their eligibility for the National Register of Historic Places. The authors dismissed the significance of one structure out of hand because it was too new (built in the 1990s) and because it was a monument (monuments are not usually found eligible for the National Register). They were right in their technical analyses, but it might have behooved them to note that the monument was to military people killed or missing in action, and it stood on the grounds of a veterans' medical center. If someone proposed to demolish that monument, and blithely told the veterans of the area that it was OK because the thing wasn't eligible for the National Register, the response would probably not be understanding, and consultation about whatever project required the demolition would be complicated. A wiser approach would be to acknowledge (quietly, and maybe with regret) that the monument probably is not eligible for the Register, while stressing its probable significance to the veterans who built it and recommending that any change to it be the subject of respectful consultation. Whether the law requires it or not, it would be smarter to seek agreement with the monument's protectors than to give them no option but to chain themselves to it and call in the press on the eve of its demolition.

Finally, you should simply recognize that they're *not in government*— unless of course they are, in which case it will probably be easier for you to communicate with them. Those of us who work in and around government can come to take a lot of things for granted, like hierarchical decision-making, the disproportionate power of lawyers, and the need to relate to the particular requirements of specific laws and regulations. And we mostly focus on a particular small range of laws and regulations. A lot of people who do NEPA work have thin and exotic notions of what NHPA is, for instance, while NHPA specialists have equally strange impressions of NEPA. And as the last sentence illustrates, we tend to make liberal use of acronyms and terms of art (see Appendix 1 if you're getting confused). Most people outside government don't take the same things for granted; they don't live in our world. Like it or not, you have to try to consult with them in *their* world, and try to keep your own in perspective.

If you're not representing the sponsor or responsible agency, and want to be consulted, you have every right[6] to insist that your schedules, financial limitations, and needs be respected, and that things be made understandable to you. Don't let anyone tell you that they're forbidden by law to hold meetings outside business hours, or on weekends—or if they tell you that, insist that they show you the law that forbids it. If you don't understand some piece of jargon or government-speak, say so, and ask that it be translated into English. If you don't like the way a meeting is structured, or information is (or is not) disseminated, speak up. Put your complaints into the public record, and if there's an oversight agency to which you can appeal, do it. In the United States, it never hurts (though it won't necessarily help) to keep your senator or congressperson informed of any roadblocks you're running into.

Deadlines

The sponsor may be in a hurry to get a decision made about the project. The last thing he or she wants to do is wait around for people to send in comments, or to resolve problems in the course of consultation. And the responsible agency may have higher authorities, or members of Congress, breathing down its neck. So there may be a lot of pressure to establish and maintain tight deadlines on comments and consultation. That's perfectly understandable, and it may even be that deadlines are established in law, or through litigation, or that they're enshrined in unalterable policy. If you're in a position to, though, you still ought to be careful about laying down hard and fast, "speak now or forever hold your peace" deadlines.

It may literally be impossible for a consulting party to meet such a deadline. They may have to talk with a dozen community elders who live back in the hills and don't come out very often or encourage visitors. They may have family, governmental, work, or ritual obligations that conflict. What may seem a perfectly reasonable deadline to government and corporate executives may seem quite unreasonable to them.

Even if it's not unreasonable, setting down an absolute deadline may be offensive; it may seem autocratic, dictatorial, and "who the hell are you, ostensible public servant or seeker of government largesse, to be slapping deadlines on me, the public?" It can get the conversation off on a bad footing.

The court in *Quechan* repeatedly noted that the government had imposed deadlines on the Tribe, and pointed out that the government—not the Tribe—had the authority to flex them to accommodate effective consultation. The government's inflexibility about deadlines clearly contributed to the record that persuaded the court to enjoin the government's decision. This is basic: the responsible agency can flex deadlines; nobody else can. If you represent an agency that has such authority, you ought to consider it.

If you must set a deadline—and you probably do, at least implicitly— then try to propose it gently, with understanding for the people you're seeking to consult. "It would be most helpful to us if you could give us your response within 45 days or so." Sure, that doesn't establish an absolute drop-dead date, after which you can pretend that responses never happened, but you may well not be able to make absolute drop-dead dates stick anyway. So, why risk alienating people by imposing them, especially if you don't absolutely need to?

If the Consultation Will Be Government-to-Government

If you're representing an agency initiating government-to-government consultation with an Indian tribal government in the United States, then there are some special things to think about when seeking views, such as:

Who Do You Contact? Almost invariably, the U.S. government agency should contact the head of the other government—for instance, the Chairperson of the tribal council. But you need to consider that the tribal or other government may be very small and strapped for funds, and it may be very easy for a communication to go astray and be buried. So if you know (or can find out) that there are specific offices within the government that are particularly relevant to the consultation (e.g., environmental office, historic preservation office, cultural committee), you ought to send copies of your correspondence to them, and maybe call them up to let them know what's coming. And try to be up to date; tribal and similar governments change frequently, and the changes aren't necessarily very well reported in the mainstream (or other) media. Most tribes do have websites, however, that will give you reasonably current data on the tribe's leadership. Many states in the western U.S. also have tribal affairs offices that keep track of changes in tribal governments.

Who Makes Contact? The general rule in government-to-government consultation is that a line officer in the federal agency—someone in the chain of command that runs back to the president—does or at least oversees consultation with the tribal government. That means someone like the regional director, or the district manager, or the field office superintendent; it does not mean the staff environmentalist, the staff archaeologist, or the staff planner. Nor does it mean a private contractor working for the agency, or an applicant for the agency's land or assistance. All those parties may become involved in consultation, and some of them may take part in figuring out who and how to consult, but a line officer needs to be demonstrably in charge. It's the line officer who should sign letters, and usually take part in initial meetings, though she and the other government's leaders may then agree to let their staffs work things out for their approval.

Coordination. It's worth thinking at the very outset about how government-to-government consultation will be coordinated with *non-governmental* consultation. If you're initiating consultation with an Indian tribal government in the United States, you may find that the tribal government wants to be consulted apart from all other parties, perhaps before others are consulted, or perhaps afterwards, or at some specified times in between. Its leadership may need direction from its legislative body—usually a tribal council—before it can begin consultation. It may require a formal tribal council resolution (the equivalent of legislation) in order to frame its views.

It may or may not want elders, religious societies, or other non-governmental tribal members to take part. It may be necessary to make a formal presentation to the tribal council or some other governmental body, or it may not. The bottom line is that you can't just treat a tribal government the way you'd treat a local historical society or a national environmental group.

At the same time, you can't let government-to-government consultation prevent the sponsor or responsible agency from consulting the historical society, the environmental group, or the tribal elders who don't agree with the tribal government. They're citizens, and they have rights too; they're just somewhat different rights from those of a tribal government, and they may have to be addressed separately. As you begin to reach out to potential consulting parties, it's wise to start thinking about how these disparate government and non-government parties can best be consulted. But understand, too, that you may need to adapt your methods as the consultation proceeds.

Sharing Information

In deciding what information to share with potential consulting parties, remember the Golden Rule. If someone were asking *you* to consult about a project, what information would you want them to provide to you? You'd probably want a nice clear map showing where the project might happen—and what alternative locations are under consideration. If there was a consultant's report on what the effects of the project might be (though there shouldn't be, if you're just starting to consider the project), you'd probably want that. You'd probably want something explaining the reasons for the project, and any constraints on what alternatives could be considered. So if you're responsible for sending information to consulting parties, send them the same kinds of information you'd want.

You also need to think about what information to request from them. The basic rule should be "as little as possible." As the *Pueblo of Sandia* case illustrated, it's not their job to give you a map of the places that are important to them, with their boundaries all neatly drawn in red ink or pixels. When you're initiating consultation, most times all you need to ask them is whether, how, when and where they'd like to consult.

At the same time, don't spurn information others do provide simply because it isn't quite what you asked for. Sandia Pueblo wouldn't tell the Forest Service where all its specific important places were, but it did send in a tribal council resolution saying that the whole canyon was significant. Such a resolution is the equivalent of an act of Congress, and the Forest Service should have given it close attention. Instead it just filed it, and that negligence helped convince the court that it had acted in bad faith.

Don't assume you know what information the consultation will require, and set out to gather it before consultation has begun. One U.S. agency we know routinely has archaeological surveys done as one of the first steps in its EIA process. Then it gets into arguments with consulting parties about who gets access to the survey results, and whether the survey was adequate. But archaeological survey is often irrelevant to the issues of concern to the consulting parties, so everyone winds up arguing about more or less peripheral matters. This is why the NHPA Section 106 regulations require consultation when determining the *scope* of an effort to identify historic properties. It's only sensible to discuss what you need to find out about an area before you commit time and money to finding it out.

If you're a potential consulting party who's contacted by an agency or sponsor, be careful about asking them for too much or too specific information. Indian tribes in the U.S. often make the mistake of telling agencies that they want to receive things like "cultural resource" survey reports when consultation is initiated. But if the agency or sponsor is initiating consultation early in planning, there won't be any survey reports yet; consultation is about what reports—if any—need to be prepared, what sorts of studies—if any—are needed. By asking for reports, the tribe is essentially giving up its chance to consult about whether and how such reports should be produced, and what they should address.

Inviting People to Consult

An invitation to consult is usually sent out in the form of a letter, or sometimes as an email. In Appendix 2A we dissect a real letter sent by a federal agency, ostensibly inviting people to consult. Here, let's just offer a few recommendations and try a thought experiment.

Tell them what you're trying to do, up front. Don't make the recipient wade through several paragraphs of text before she finds out what you're writing about.

Minimize government-speak. Try to avoid a lot of citations to laws, regulations, guidelines and standards. You may need a few, but rigorously excise those that don't bear directly on what you're doing or asking.

Minimize jargon. Don't assume that those receiving your letter will know a FONSI from a fuzzy bear, or what it means to have "no adverse effect" on a "historic property."

Avoid offensive terms. A group of people concerned about a place where their ancestors lived, worshipped, or were buried may be offended by having the place called an "archaeological site," so consider calling it something else. Is this being politically correct? Sure, and there's a practical reason for political correctness; if you use language that makes people mad before you even start talking, that's an impediment to productive consultation.

Use active voice if you can. "The Bureau of Fish and Flowers proposes to dig a fish pond," is better than "It is proposed that a fish pond be dug." "We understand that the pueblo is historically and culturally important," beats "It is believed that the pueblo possesses historic and cultural significance."

Thought experiment. Look at the following letter—a real one only mildly modified here to avoid seeming to disrespect its authors—and think about how to improve it.

Dear Mr. Smith:

The Bureau of Fish and Flowers (BFF) would like to notify you about a Public Fishing Enhancement (PFE) project (the "Undertaking") within the Sport Fishing Augmentation and Improvement (SFAI) initiative taking place on public lands south of the Town of Townley, East Dakota. The SFAI initiative is a BFF strategic effort to identify and improve potential public fishing areas in support of BFF's goal to increase fish consumption and expand sport fishing.

Too many acronyms? Too many terms of art? Is it clear what's proposed?

BFF's PFE authority expired on December 31, 2012. In anticipation of the sunset of our legislative authority, BFF entered into a PFE agreement with Gillslit Anglers, Inc. (permittee) before December 31, 2012 by utilizing a modified process that BFF created specifically for this purpose. The PFE contains only the basic transaction terms, and identifies project milestone action items and deliverables with dates for completion that the parties must conduct and evaluate—including all historic preservation studies and any subsequent requirements to comply—and bring to resolution and conclusion. Once all steps are satisfied, completed and properly documented within the milestones established, BFF will finalize negotiations with the permittee with the goal of executing an underlying Amended & Restated PFE at a later date to be determined. Please note that the PFE using the modified process was not a federal action. The federal action will occur with the signing of the Amended & Restated PFE.

Do the consulting parties really need to know all this? Does it contribute to understanding of the project or its possible impacts? Is it clear? Does it raise unnecessary questions? Are there too many terms of art? Do we yet know what's actually proposed?

The Townley PFE project team is now working towards the completion of project milestone action items and deliverables that must be completed prior to the execution of the Amended & Restated PFE. As a requirement of successful completion of the PFE, BFF and the permittee must fulfill their responsibilities under Section 106 of the National Historic Preservation Act (NHPA) for the Undertaking. With this said the East Dakota Division of Historic Places (WDHP) under a request pursuant to Section 106 of the National Historic Preservation Act, as amended, and its implementing regulation 36 CFR Part 800, have concurred with the determination of a 'No Adverse Impact' for this project.

Is there anything here that suggests the agency isn't consulting in a time-ly manner? They seem to be pretty sure about what they're going to do, and they've already gotten agreement with the State. Can consultation with others be meaningful at this point?

> This review decision from the WDHP, pursuant to 36 CFR Part 800, is intended to provide citizens with an opportunity to participate in the Section 106 consultation process to address the effects of this Undertaking. Please notify BFF within 30 days of the date of this letter if your organization elects to participate in this consultation.

If you received this letter, would you feel encouraged to participate?

Or would you feel that BFF was just going through the motions, sending out a letter so it could check off the "Yep, we've consulted" box on the paper-work supporting a decision it's already made? We'd feel that way too. In Appendix 2 we've included another real contact letter (again slightly edited for purposes of anonymity) that may be a better model, though again we stress that each case is unique and requires its own approach to communication with the parties.

CHAPTER 4

Discussing

Consultation means the process of... discussing... the views of other participants... (36 CFR §800.16(f))

The sponsor or agency has begun to seek the views of other parties (but remember that this search should continue throughout the course of consultation) and has found some people who want to talk. The next aspect of consultation, according to the Advisory Council's definition, is *discussing* their views.

But what if the sponsor or agency *doesn't* find anyone who wants to consult? What if nobody actually cares (and there's nobody who's required by law to consult, as the U.S. Fish and Wildlife Service is under Section 7 of the Endangered Species Act)? In most cases, truth be told, that's the situation; most things a government agency does or permits are more or less routine actions that don't bother anyone, and no one wants to take part in their review (even when, taking a long view, they probably should).

There's nothing that requires people to be interested in an agency's projects, and nothing that requires an agency or sponsor to twist people's arms to get them involved. For the sake of a project's administrative record, whoever's responsible should be able to document a reasonable, good-faith effort to *seek* people's views, but if no one wants to provide them, or if all they want to do is provide them and leave you alone to consider them, then you can document this fact and be done with it. But *do* document it, so that if a question arises later in project planning, you can show what you did and what the response was. This is not called Commendable Yeomanly Alertness, but the acronym is the same.

Exchanging Views

"Discussing" something obviously means exchanging views about it, considering such views, and trying to resolve differences of opinion about them. It's a back-and-forth, interactive process. It is *not* just a matter of sending someone a letter, providing them with a report, or issuing a notice—though all these activities may be parts of the discussion. The important thing to remember is that a discussion must be interactive. You can't have a discussion only with yourself.

So how do we go about exchanging views, and narrowing differences between them?

Discussion may be fairly free-form, or highly structured, depending on the subject, the parties, the parties' preferences, and any legal standards that apply. Generally, though, once you've found someone to consult, with views to discuss, how do you do it?

Correspondence

Much of the discussion will probably take the form of correspondence—letters, memoranda, emails, and the like. The same sorts of rules apply to correspondence during ongoing discussion that apply to initial contact letters, as addressed in the last chapter. Remember that you're trying to *communicate*, so keep your letters and emails as simple as possible—straightforward, honest, and complete. Your agency's or company's correspondence policies, or your lawyer, or your supervisor, may not let you indulge in too much clarity, completeness, or honesty, but try to do the best you can.

Those who receive correspondence from government agencies should understand—but often don't—that agency correspondence is rarely produced by a single individual. There's a rule in government that no one ever writes what she signs or signs what he writes. Correspondence is drafted and reviewed through something usually (in U.S. government parlance) called "the surname process," in which a whole range of people and offices in the agency pecking order have to "sign off" on the draft, each able to make changes or insist that changes be made. The result (if there is a result—sometimes the process becomes one of endless loops) can easily be a camel,[1] and no particular person may be responsible for its strange humps, neck shape, and poop-flinging tail. So don't be too hard on those behind such documents (unless you have a strategic reason to be), and don't assume that an idiotic letter is the product of ill intent, or even—necessarily—the product of idiots.

Of course, if you're a government agency consulting with another government agency, there are probably standard forms and formats that one or the other agency uses. Using them may facilitate communication, however exotic the documents may appear to people on the outside. Still, though, it's useful to try to be clear even in interagency correspondence, both because people outside government might review your writings (for example, in court), and because confusing one another doesn't make for efficient government.

Setting Up Meetings

By "meetings," we mean both the traditional face-to-face sit-downs around a table and such things as conference calls, webinars, and videoconferences. We suggest trying to avoid having meetings for their own sake. Everyone's busy, everyone has work to do, and holding a meeting just because it's the routine thing to do wastes everybody's time. It may irritate, even infuriate your consulting partners. On the other hand, some people and groups expect a meeting, and feel disrespected if one isn't held—even if there doesn't seem to be much reason for one. Some regulations and agency procedures require that meetings be held, regardless of need.

Moreover, there's a lot to be said for hashing things out face-to-face. Certainly where big, complex issues are to be discussed, or if you're trying for the kind of collaborative problem-solving espoused by Innes and Booher (2010)—as they stress, face-to-face interaction is vital. We don't for a moment mean to discourage meetings; we just want to encourage trying to make them meaningful. On balance, if you're not sure whether a meeting is needed, you probably ought to organize one, or at least discuss doing so with your consulting partners.

If you *do* have meetings to arrange, try to make them convenient for everyone. Here are some variables to consider:

Date, Time, and Venue   "Convenience" is mostly a matter of time and place. Try to schedule meetings on dates and at times when all those—or at least most of those—with whom you're consulting can attend. And schedule them in places that work for them. This will, of course, require some pre-meeting coordination both with those you're inviting to attend and with those who control the venue.

Some common constraints on *timing* include:

- Work schedules (In the U.S., evenings and weekends tend to be best);
- Holidays—national, religious, regional, local, tribal;
- Family considerations (When can people get away from their children, or family members for whom they're caretakers? What other family obligations may conflict?); and
- Conflicting community events (other meetings, pow-wows in Indian country, fishing and harvest schedules, religious events, hunting seasons).

Some common *venue* issues include:

- Geographic convenience; how easy is it to get to the venue by various modes of transportation?
- Social convenience; will anyone feel uncomfortable about meeting in the venue? Does it carry symbolic freight for any of the consulting parties ("Everybody knows about the soundproof torture chambers in the basement!")
- Size of the venue: will it accommodate everyone who may come?
- Shape and organization of the venue; some venues (e.g. auditoria) are organized for passive watching and listening, while others are better for interaction. Some venues have space for break-out sessions; others don't. What do you need?
- Openness to the public: how open do the consulting parties *want* it to be? If they don't want it to be very open (as is not infrequently the case where sensitive cultural issues may come up), how *closed* can it be made without violating relevant laws or regulations, or infuriating those shut out? What options are available for balancing openness with protecting confidentiality?
- Access by media: do the consulting parties want media access, or not? And whatever they want, how do you balance the rights and duties of the media and the desires of people who are sensitive about being seen, heard, or reported on?
- Access by the handicapped;
- Access to translation and other services; and
- Availability of places to eat, and lodging places.

Cost   Meetings cost money—not only for whoever's renting or otherwise providing the venue, but for everyone who participates. They involve taking time off work, paying for gas or air fares, maybe hotel rooms and restaurant meals. People may not like to acknowledge it, but the cost of taking part in meetings may be a real impediment to consultation, particularly by low income communities and groups. It's notable that in each of the relatively successful collaborative efforts discussed by Innes and Booher (2010), someone had to underwrite some substantial costs.

Even where all involved are willing to try, dealing with cost issues can be tricky. It may be embarrassing for a low income group to volunteer the fact that its representatives can't afford to attend a meeting, and the same group may understandably be uncomfortable about accepting financial help from, say, the project sponsor or responsible agency, for fear of being perceived to have been "bought." Despite a long-standing executive order[2] and various implementing procedures and agreements about accommodating participation by low income and minority groups, many U.S. government agencies have policies prohibiting or strictly limiting expenditures on helping outside parties participate in consultation.

How many of these and other issues you may need to worry about will depend on the project, how controversial it is, the parties involved, the relevant geography, and a host of other particular factors. Whatever they are, you need to think about them in advance, to avoid setting up a meeting that's doomed to futility before it even starts.

Setting Up a Meeting Room   For an exchange of views, auditorium or traditional classroom seating is seldom effective. Rows of seats facing a podium are fine for a briefing, a lecture, or an undergraduate lecture class, but such a layout does nothing to encourage or even permit interaction. Usually you'll want the parties gathered around a table, or around a set of tables arranged in a circle, oval, or rectangle, or in an open-ended "U" arrangement.

Some consulting parties may have definite preferences as to the shape of the room or its seating. The circle, for example, has special cultural/spiritual significance to many American Indian tribes and other indigenous groups, and may be such a group's preferred (or *not* preferred) arrangement.

Of course, much depends on how the meeting itself will be organized. For instance:

- Will there be presentations with slides or other projected graphics? Then you'll need access to the projector—though forcing presenters to crawl under encircling tables to get to it *can* be something of an ice-breaker.

- Will there be a facilitator? If so, where will he position himself; how will she move around the room?

- Do you need space for whiteboards, maps, other graphics? Will you want to write things down on butcher paper and post them up on the walls? If so, is this allowed in your preferred venue?

- Will you want to break up into smaller groups, or allow for caucuses? If so, you need separate space(s) where this can happen.

- Will you have people participating by telephone, or via the internet? Although the technology for such inclusion is improving all the time, in 2013 it's still the case that telephone participants tend to become forgotten voices and ears in little black thingies in the middle of the table. You'll need to think about how they can be helped to hear, and be heard. If you're going to have a videoconference so the remote participants actually can be seen as well as heard, this will influence the arrangement of your room(s).

- Should you provide snacks, coffee, or other refreshments? In some communities it is almost unheard of not to, but in some agencies it's hard to get it approved, or funded. In our experience it's not uncommon for the individual running or facilitating the meeting to provide refreshments out of his or her own pocket, which isn't very fair but may be the only option.

More Substantial Feeding   Particularly if you're dealing with an indigenous or other more or less traditional community, having lunch or other substantial refreshments may be in order. Exactly what sort of feeding opportunity may be appropriate varies widely from group to group, and of course the responsible agency may have rules about what it can and cannot provide. But it's another thing to look into. Particularly in relatively traditional communities, a fairly substantial feeding—say, a full buffet lunch—may break a lot of ice. Of course, you need to think about the food preferences and requirements of your participants; ham sandwiches are a poor choice if a lot of your participants are Muslim or Jewish. And you probably don't want to go overboard, lest you be accused of trying to buy favors with *foie gras.*

If you're one of the parties being consulted by a sponsor or agency, it may be beneficial to provide and organize the venue, particularly if you have ready access to one that's suitable from your point of view (say, your tribal council building). This puts everyone on your turf, playing (to some extent at least) by your rules, and it's probably more convenient for you than holding the meeting somewhere else. It may cost some money, but so would bussing your people in to the capital city.

Preparing Yourself

It's important to prepare yourself, your team, your colleagues or organizational superiors for the meeting. If you want it to go well, you can't treat it as just another item on your calendar. You need to get ready for it, and think some things through.

Being Informed   Prepare for the meeting, if you can, by getting a good handle not only on the topic you're meeting about, but on related topics—or things that may not seem related to you but that can affect the course of the discussion. What other projects have been the subjects of consultation in the area in the last few decades? What other projects or actions of government have *not* been the subjects of consultation but should have been? How have the people you're meeting with been affected by, and reacted to, these actions?

You also ought to find out as much as you can about those with whom you'll be meeting. How are they organized, if they are? Who are the leaders of the groups who may take part, and what are their backgrounds? What are their likely concerns? How do they relate generally to government? To industry? To change? To your cultural values? Are there individuals or groups who are likely to grandstand? Belabor old wrongs? Introduce new ones that may or may not have anything evident to do with your consultation? Are there deep divisions among the people with whom you'll be consulting, along racial, ethnic, economic, educational, or other lines? Are there haves and have-nots? Environmental justice issues?

This recommendation, like others, applies to those being consulted as well as to those responsible for the consultation. Maybe you know all about the Bureau of Fish and Flowers, but if you don't, it's a good idea to try to get informed. Check their website; talk to others who've dealt with them. Try to understand how they're organized, how decisions are made, who calls the shots. Look into how they're funded, how they interact with other agencies and organizations. We've seen many cases in which intractable issues with a state highway agency got a lot more tractable when the Federal Highway Administration—which provides funding to the states—got involved. If you're not getting satisfaction from the local, regional, state or provincial office, you may need to go higher. Where the sponsor is non-governmental, it can be useful to know how they're organized, how they relate to other companies, who regulates them, and what issues are hot-button topics for them. In the Mole Lake Sokaogon case mentioned in Chapter 3, for example, the Ojibwe community gained a useful bargaining chip when it learned that the multinational owner of the mining company was trying to enhance its reputation for responsibility toward the environment. Knowledge *is* power.

Knowing Yourself "O, wad some Power the giftie gie us," cried Robert Burns, "To see oursels as others see us!"[3] Knowing what freight you, your associates, and your agency or organization bring to the table can be a serious challenge, but one you ought to try to confront. Consider—and discuss with your associates on your side of the table if you can—what assumptions, biases, and fears might affect your conduct during the meeting. Is your mind made up (or has it been made up for you) about the project, its impacts, and what ought to be done? Do you or others on your team have attitudes toward other consulting parties that need to be taken into account? Problems with others' means of expressing themselves? With their race, color, ethnicity, religion, or sexual orientation? With their attitudes as you understand them? You probably can't change your biases (whether they're justified or not), but if you honestly acknowledge them, at least to yourself, you'll be better able to control them during the meeting.

If nothing else, try to imagine yourself in the shoes of the people with whom you're consulting. How are they likely to see you; how are they likely to interpret what you say? No one's going to give you Burns' giftie, but you can try, yourself, to imagine it.

This is not to say that you need to make nice with everyone. If you're in danger of having your treasured environment trashed, you probably don't feel like being nice, and if you're too nice, the sponsor or agency may think you're a pushover. But your use of anger, sarcasm, bitterness, and insults should be calibrated; think about when, where, and how they may be useful to you, and deploy them accordingly. (Nissley chuckles when King says this, since it's a rule he's never learned to follow.)

Composition of your Team   Think about the team you're bringing to the table, and how its members will be perceived by the other consulting parties. Try not to have so many people that you seem to be trying to overpower, or gang up, but try to have *enough* people, and the *right* people, to cover all the necessary bases. Are you a historical society allied with an indigenous group and environmentalists? You need all three to be represented by people who are at least generally able to speak for them and who've worked out some sort of game plan in advance. Are you the project sponsor? Make sure you have managerial, legal, and technical expertise on your team so that questions can be answered and misapprehensions corrected. Though sometimes it's unavoidable, or strategically desirable, it's usually best to avoid having to say "I'll get back to you about that."

Lawyers and Expert Consultants   Consultation meetings typically occur in response to some set of laws or regulations, and it's a very, very good idea to have someone on your team who understands what they are and how they work. If you don't, and those with whom you're consulting do, you're likely to get bamboozled. On the other hand, it's usually unwise to leave the consultation entirely to the lawyers. They should be telling you and your consulting partners what the legal requirements are, and the legal implications of taking various courses of action; they should not define what's desirable or acceptable as an outcome. And of course, not every lawyer is expert in all kinds of law. Similarly, consultation shouldn't be left to expert consultants. We can advise, we can facilitate, we can help in a wide variety of ways, but however expert we may be and whatever our areas of expertise are, we're not you, and you—not we—are going to have to live with the outcome.

Dress and Adornment   The clothes you wear and the things with which you adorn yourself can send messages, so you ought to select them with some care. Consider things like:

- Uniform or civilian clothes? If you sometimes wear a uniform, is it appropriate to wear it, or would civvies be better?

- How formal? If civvies are the rule (or all you wear), how formal should they be? This varies widely with the situation—what's typically expected in the region, under circumstances like those in which you're consulting?

- What about adornments? If you're consulting with an Indian tribe or other indigenous group, it's usually not a good idea to dress in imitation of what you think is their traditional garb. Don't wear feathers or strings of beads, for instance, at least if you're male. But if you normally wear such things, and/or you have something that has meaning to those you're consulting with, like the abalone shell necklace they gave you last year during another consultation, wearing it *may* be appropriate and positive. If you're military and have a chest-full of medals, it may or may not be a good idea to wear them; think about the impression you're trying to convey. If you have tattoos, think about their symbolism, or what others may interpret as their symbolism. Covering them up may seem like an affront to your self-expression, but it may facilitate communication.

- Armed or disarmed? This is pretty much a no-brainer. Even if it's perfectly legal, even if you think you have the right to, and even if you routinely carry a sidearm (supposing you're a park ranger or police officer, for example), don't wear it to a consultation. It will almost inevitably convey an impression of disproportionate power and coercive intent.

Having a Plan   Have at least a rough idea of how you'd like the meeting to go. What topics need to be covered? Which ones should be first? Second? Third? How much time should be allotted to each? How should breaks be scheduled? And particularly, where do you and your associates want to come out at the end of the meeting? What are your objectives?

On the other hand, it's unwise to be a slave to your plan. Consultation is a two-way street, and you need to be able and willing to change the agenda as needed, or as opportunities arise. In other words, have a plan, but not too rigid a plan. You particularly should be alert to, and ready to deal with, issues that your consulting partners bring to the table that *they* think are important but you may not have considered or given much weight.

Plan versus Agenda   Your *plan* obviously needs to be your own; only you and those you represent can decide what you want to get out of the meeting and how to get it. But the meeting *agenda* needs to be worked out with the other consulting parties. When you're discussing date, time, and venue with the other consulting parties, you ought to talk about the agenda, too. What topics do *they* want discussed? This is another of those simple, obvious matters whose handling is critical to getting the consultation off on a good foot. All too often, in our experience, project sponsors and responsible agencies think they *know* what the agenda has to be, based on standard templates (explicit or implicit) or just on the issues as they frame them. Other participants may see things very differently, and if they're not consulted about the agenda they may feel that the agency or sponsor doesn't care about their concerns. So certainly make your own plans, but develop the agenda as cooperatively as possible. And be prepared to adjust your plans as the agenda develops.

If you're one of the parties being consulted, don't automatically buy into whatever agenda the agency or sponsor lays down, and think about developing your own agenda for the meeting—even if you don't make it public.

Interests, Not Positions   One of the most important guidelines given in the classic dispute resolution guidebook, *Getting to Yes* (Fisher, Ury & Patton 2011) is to seek the *interests* that underlie *positions*. Positions tend to be non-negotiable ("We have to build our wind energy project *here*"), while the interests that drive them ("We need a windy place for our project") allow more negotiating room. We'll return to this guideline as we go along. In preparing for a meeting, it will be helpful for you to consider your own positions and think about what interests justify them. And try, if you can, to get the other members of your team to do the same—especially those who call your team's shots. They're the ones who define the positions you have to take, and they ought to be able to articulate the interests that drive them. We realize that this may be a serious challenge—the boss may not want to be challenged by an underling about why the project has to be built right here—but you'll get a lot farther in consultation, a lot faster, with a lot less misery, if your whole team can minimize position-taking and emphasize the articulation of interests.

The term "interest-based consultation" is getting a good deal of use in government and industry guidance on consultation with indigenous groups (c.f. Solvit 2010). Sometimes it clearly means seeking out and addressing interests, while in other cases the words "interest" and "based" seem simply to be tossed in front of "consultation" with no particular meaning intended. We suggest not being satisfied with just using the words. The actual process of really seeking interests under positions can have very fruitful results.

It's a process that everyone can take part in. In simplest terms, it means asking "why" and "why not?" Why must the wind generators be on this hill and not on some other hill? Why do we really need these generators, anyway? Why not generate the power we need by covering all the town's warehouses with solar panels? The sponsor ought to be able to answer such questions, and explain what interests drive the answers given, and it's perfectly reasonable for consulting parties to ask them and demand answers.

It's as important for non-sponsor consulting parties to be clear about their interests as it is for the sponsor to be. Why do you *not* want the wind turbines on the hill? What do you find offensive about them and why? This may seem so blazingly obvious that you shouldn't have to explain it, but you probably do. It will also be useful to you, yourselves, to be clear in your minds about your interests. We have seen cases in which a party has won the day, prevailed upon a sponsor to change a project to fix whatever it was the party agreed to, and the party has gone on fighting, not quite recognizing the win. Which may have meant that they hadn't really won because they'd failed to make their real interests clear, or that they *had* won but were so fixated on the position of being in opposition that they just couldn't quit.

Conducting Meetings

Most of us who work with project planning are used to having meetings that follow a rather standard pattern. Whoever is hosting the meeting speaks first, welcoming everyone, outlining the gathering's purposes, setting the ground rules. Then there may be a presentation by a project sponsor, or agency staff who've reviewed the project. Then other official representatives of agencies and organizations may speak, or maybe any politicians who are taking part. Then there's an open discussion, then someone summarizes what's happened, and the meeting's brought to a close. We get so used to this format that we may come to assume it's the way meetings have to be.

Others, though, may have quite different ideas about how a meeting is to be conducted. This is, of course, especially the case when we're consulting in a non-Euroamerican cultural context, or across cultural boundaries. For instance, if we're having a meeting in the traditional territory of an Indian tribe (hard not to do in the continental United States or Canada), tribal members may think that the first to speak should be a representative of the tribe on whose erstwhile land we're meeting. They may not make much of this preference, but it may sour the discussion if we fail to ask the appropriate tribal representative to speak at the beginning of the meeting. Conversely, making such a request may get the whole discussion off on a better foot.

More common among tribes and some other traditional communities is the wish for the meeting to begin, and possibly to end, with a prayer, rendered by an appropriate spiritual leader, often in a native language. This may offend our Euroamerican preference for keeping "church" and "state" separate, but we ought to remember that each daily session of the U.S. Senate and House of Representatives begins with a prayer presided over by a chaplain. It may be tricky to accommodate the wish for a prayer, though, because somebody needs first to find out (a) whether a prayer is desired, and if so, (b) who will say it. And it may be that no one will volunteer. This is something you need to work out if you can through pre-meeting consultation.

Other structural guidelines to consider include:

- Asking community elders to speak first, and being understanding if they do not wish to speak or ask that another representative—maybe younger and more articulate in English or whatever the language of the majority is—speak for them;

- Scheduling breaks to accommodate the elderly, the infirm, or those who want to get a cigarette or caucus with their colleagues;

- *Not* having set-piece presentations by government officials or the project sponsor, or at least trying to keep them strictly controlled as to time. It can be extremely frustrating to attend a meeting where you expect to be able to speak your piece, and even negotiate with others, and then have most of the time taken up by officials blabbing on about project details that can be more efficiently addressed in other ways, or mouthing platitudes that nobody believes anyway. On the other hand, everyone does need to understand what's being proposed, and should be able to ask questions and get answers. Think about how to provide the information needed in a way that respects everyone's time and interests.

Using a Facilitator

A facilitator is a more or less outside, more or less disinterested party who is brought in to manage a meeting and try to bring it to a mutually agreeable conclusion. Facilitation has become a popular part of many twenty-first century consultations. Many people practice facilitation—both of us have done so at various times, and may again. There are organizations of facilitators (and mediators, arbitrators, etc.) that prescribe recommended practices and promulgate codes of ethics.[4]

The advantage of using a facilitator is that his or her job is simply to keep the meeting on track and make everybody feel like they've had a fair shake. The facilitator in theory doesn't care about the outcome of the meeting (or series of meetings), just about the integrity of the process and how satisfied the participants are with it. Particularly in a contentious consultation, a facilitator may be very helpful in avoiding gridlock and in keeping the parties talking to (and not past) one another. Facilitation may also help all the participants give fair consideration to new ideas and overcome institutional biases.

On the other hand, because he or she almost by definition has no background in the project under review, and often little or no expertise in the laws and regulations under which the consultation occurs, the facilitator may be the least knowledgeable person in the room, quite incapable of distinguishing fact from fiction, wheat from chaff. You may wind up spending a lot of time educating the facilitator—which may compromise, or be perceived to compromise, the facilitator's objectivity. Or the facilitator, in the interests of fairness, may let the meeting get dragged off down rabbit holes by people pursuing personal agendas or impossible solutions. And the people who are most demanding of the facilitator's time, and most likely to drag him or her (and thereby the meeting) off into the weeds may not be the people most affected by and concerned about your project. The people who *are* most affected and concerned may find it very frustrating to have to sit politely and listen to discussions of what are to them very marginal issues, or issues that they know have been beaten to death in other contexts. An experienced facilitator should have learned to be alert to diversions, and to make use of the expertise in the room without letting anybody run off with the meeting, but it's always a chancy business.

Ideally, a facilitator ought to be engaged by parties on all, or both, sides of the table, so he or she doesn't seem to be the tool of his or her employer.

But since the project sponsor is usually the one with the money, this sort of balance may be hard to achieve. There may be ways to have an impartial third party provide the facilitator, and at the very least, the consulting parties ought to agree on the facilitator and his or her scope of services.

So by all means consider using a facilitator, and maybe shop around for one whose price is right and who seems to have an appropriate mix of knowledge and skills, but don't assume that he or she is going to make everything right. In most cases you probably don't want to start out with a facilitator; it may be better to see how far you can get without one, bringing one in only if consultation gets bogged down.

Listening Session

Another popular twenty-first-century twist on consultation meetings (and other kinds of get-togethers) is the "listening session." A listening session is a meeting in which the people with the power—in our case usually the project sponsor and/or the responsible federal and state agencies—organize the meeting but in effect become the audience, ostensibly listening to whatever concerns people bring up. There's a widespread and to some extent justified perception that listening sessions are more respectful of people's interests than are more traditional forms of consultation.

In his website discussion of listening sessions, executive coach Tony Mayo wisely (we think) emphasizes that "listening is important [but] action makes the difference" (Mayo n.d.). It's seriously disrespectful just to listen to what people say, nod respectfully, shake everybody's hand and walk away, particularly if things then proceed without any response to what people have told you. A listening session may be useful, but it's no substitute for consultation that actually seeks to define and resolve people's concerns. If you hold a listening session, try to be sure that once it's over, the listeners don't just say "Whew, that's over," and go on as though nothing had happened. Try to make sure that something comes out of the session, that something is done in response to what was said.

Meetings Outside of Meetings

Formal, organized, all-party meetings are not the only means of discussing issues during consultation. Besides correspondence by letter and email, it also may be perfectly appropriate to meet one-on-one with one or more other consulting parties—provided you don't violate rules against *ex parte* communication, and provided your one-on-one meetings don't thwart the purposes of consultation.

Ex parte communication rules vary from jurisdiction to jurisdiction, but they generally prohibit off-the-record communication with a decision maker. Communications must be shared, or at least sharable, with all parties to an action. Even if you're not technically subject to an *ex parte* prohibition, appearing to be trying to influence the decision maker through back doors and in smoke-filled rooms is not going to encourage other consulting parties to trust you. However, there is nothing to keep consulting parties *other than* the decision maker's representatives from engaging in all the bilateral, trilateral, or multilateral discussions they wish, among themselves. And in most cases, one-on-one communication with the decision maker's representatives is OK as long as it's on the record.

Confidentiality

Consultation is sometimes impeded when one party keeps important information confidential, neglecting or refusing to share it with the other parties. This may be done secretly, of course, without any acknowledgement that a piece of information (say, about a historic place or an environmental impact) exists, but when it's acknowledged it is often justified—supposedly—in one or more of five ways:

1. *It's proprietary.* Proprietary information is information a private company owns and wants to keep to itself, usually based on the contention that holding onto it gives the company an advantage in the marketplace. Data on inventions by a company's laboratories are often and understandably held to be proprietary. However, sometimes a company may designate as proprietary certain information developed by its employees or contractors that might be used to raise questions about a project the company proposes. Releasing such data arguably would put the company in a disadvantageous market position, so there's some basis for thinking of it as proprietary, but keeping it secret obviously frustrates open consultation about things like environmental impacts. We can't say how often this kind of thing happens; the "its proprietary" argument is probably

made much more often within a company or between a company and its contractors than it is in public discussions, but we have encountered examples of it over the years.

2. *It will be misused.* A common excuse for keeping information confidential is that it will be misused by irresponsible segments of the public. A classic example of this excuse lies in the very common practice of keeping data on archaeological sites and other "cultural resources" confidential, sharing such data only with "qualified professionals" approved by a federal or state agency. There is, of course, some merit to this excuse; irresponsible people do sometimes dig up archaeological sites, cut rock art off cave walls, and vandalize historic buildings. But it can also be self-serving on the part of an agency or project sponsor—keeping information out of the hands of consulting parties who might use it to challenge a planned project. The practice particularly raises eyebrows when applied to people closely associated with the information: "Yes, we collected all this information from you, or about your ancestors, or on your land, but we can't share it with you because you might misuse it." It may be possible to make this stick legally, but it does nothing good for the quality of consultation.

3. *An indigenous group wants it kept secret.* Indian tribes and other indigenous groups often do want information kept secret on sensitive aspects of the environment—for example, information bearing on ancestral burial places, spiritual activities and beliefs, places thought to have spiritual power or sensitivity, and culturally important plants, animals, or minerals. But particularly when a non-indigenous group (e.g. a government agency) says it must keep information confidential on this basis, it's a good idea to try to find out what the indigenous group really wants. And the indigenous group itself needs to think about what kinds of information it *can* share, because it really is hard to consult about something that's unknown.

4. *Releasing it is forbidden by law.* This excuse is usually combined with one or more of the two previous excuses. In the U.S., one or both of two legal standards tend to be cited: One is Section 9 of the federal Archaeological Resources Protection Act (ARPA); the other is Section 304 of the National

Historic Preservation Act (NHPA). Actually, neither law forbids release of information. Section 9 of ARPA *allows* a federal agency to keep information on "archaeological resources" confidential *if* such resources (archaeological sites, artifacts, etc.) are on federal or Indian tribal land and the agency determines that releasing information could lead to their loss or destruction; it's a discretionary provision. Section 304 of NHPA *does* mandate that information on "historic properties" be kept confidential under some circumstances, but only if the relevant agency, in consultation with the Secretary of the Interior, finds that one of the legally specified circumstances exists. And in such a case, the Secretary's representative (the Keeper of the National Register of Historic Places) gets to determine what information can be released, and to whom, for purposes of activities like project review. Agencies and project sponsors—and archaeological consultants—quite commonly gloss over these fine points and just insist that "the law" requires that data on historic places be kept secret. That's simply not true.

5. *It's pre-decisional or only in draft.* Many freedom of information laws excuse government agencies from releasing documents to the public if they're "pre-decisional"—that is, developed to inform or support a decision that's not yet been made. A related argument for keeping a document secret is that it's a draft; we'll share it when it's finalized but not before. We know of one case in which a government agency repeatedly refused over a period of several years to share information with an Indian tribe—some 1200 pages of information, on 463 recorded cultural sites created by the tribe's ancestors—because the report was in draft. Here again, it may be possible to construct a legal and policy-based argument for such secrecy, but one ought to consider what impact it will have on consultation.

Even if secrecy is justified, it gets in the way of consultation, and it's worth thinking about ways to balance the need for it against the need to share information. Are some portions of sensitive data safe to release? Can confidential data be released conditionally, subject to protective rules and standards? Can data be shared confidentially with some parties and not others? There may be fine lines to be drawn, thin hairs to be split, but it's important to try to find ways to avoid letting secrecy—even when justified—thwart the purposes of consultation.

What to Discuss?

The substance of each consultation is naturally case-specific, but you can usually expect to discuss some or all of the following topics:

- What's proposed?
- Why is it proposed?
- What alternatives are there that would achieve the same or similar purposes?
- What problems, if any, does anyone have with the proposal and/or its alternatives?
- What kinds of impacts may the project and alternatives have on the environment—that is, on the land, air, water, on plants and animals, on whatever cultural values people invest in the environment, on human land use, on the local economy?
- What can be done about the problems and impacts, if any?
- Can we do things to make the final project plan positive for the consulting parties?

If you're consulting under a resource-specific law like the Endangered Species Act or the NHPA, you may want, or be directed, to keep the discussion focused very tightly on the subject of the law—on endangered species and their habitats, on historic places as defined by the National Park Service. Trying to keep the discussion within narrow boundaries may well be fruitless, however—particularly if you're talking with real people in real communities, not just with fellow bureaucrats in other government agencies. At least where laws like NHPA are the bases for consultation, we suggest not trying to keep things too tightly focused. Remember Queen Elizabeth's two reasons for consultation—learning things you don't know, and building agreement. You won't learn new things (including new things about subjects you think you understand) if you exclude things from discussion. And you won't build consensus if you demean people by suggesting that what they want to talk about isn't important.

Of course, if someone wants to talk about what he was told by the folks from Alpha Centauri who abducted him to their hovering spacecraft, it's reasonable to encourage him—politely—to take his topic elsewhere. But be careful. If a lot of people believe that the spacecraft landed in an area that will be affected by your project, that belief—or others related to it somehow— may have given special value to the landing area in the eyes of the community. There may be a reason for this that you ought to consider. Maybe a spacecraft really did land there, or maybe the spacecraft story is the latest version of a longer-standing cultural tradition about the place, which may in turn reflect peculiarities about the place that people have felt compelled to interpret. And whether there's anything "to" the spacecraft story or not, if people believe it, or just feel like the area has something special about it, those public attitudes are things you'll have to deal with one way or another if planning for the project proceeds.

If you're the group that wants to discuss protecting the place where the spacecraft landed—or your community's traditional swimming hole, or the Old Oak, or the old home neighborhood—you may find it difficult to convince the other parties that your subject is a worthy one. It will help if you can somehow relate it to a law, regulation, or other authoritative direction that the sponsor or oversight agency can understand, but that may require specialized expertise that you don't have, and don't have ready access to. You can also try to gain allies among other consulting parties; if they see strategic advantage in supporting you, they may do so. Here again, knowledge is power; if you don't know the laws, the regulations, the interests of other parties, you'll be at a distinct disadvantage.

Identifying Things to Discuss, and How to Discuss Them

Rather than assuming you know what ought to be discussed, it may be wise to ask your consulting partners what *they* think the topics ought to be. We're not saying to go into a discussion as a blank slate; there's nothing wrong with saying "these topics are what *we* think we need to discuss." But one way or another you ought to be open to other topics, or twists on your topics, and invite others to put their ideas on the table.

You should also be open to your consulting partners' ideas about *how* the discussion should be carried out. Should there be regular meetings? If so, how often? Where? What should the meeting format be? Should different parties host different meetings? Do we need field trips? Studies and reports? Do we need to meet at all? What alternatives are there to meetings? What information do we need? How can we get it? What constraints are there in getting or using it? Are we consulting all the right parties? Do others need to be brought in? Do we need a facilitator? A mediator? What time constraints are there? Are they reasonable; should we try to flex them? Does anybody need help in order to participate? If so, how can we provide it?

We've focused here mostly on beginning a discussion. As discussion continues, issues will get clearer and differences of perception—if not opinion—should narrow, but that narrowing is the subject of the next chapter.

Documenting What's Discussed

Starting at the very beginning—when you're first setting out to identify and engage consulting parties—you ought to start recording what happens. As you move into discussions, you need to document what topics are brought up, what opinions are expressed, what's proposed, counter-proposed, rebutted, or accepted. This is not to say that you need a court reporter in every meeting, or to record every discussion on audio or video media, but if asked two or ten or fifty years from now how the discussion went, whether Issue X was discussed and if so, whether and how it was resolved, you (or someone) ought to be able to consult your documentation and come up with an answer. And if you get run over by a truck tomorrow, your successor should have the documentary basis necessary to pick up where you left off.

Before your first meeting, you should think about the options available for recording and documenting what is said and by whom. Before the meeting, or at it, check with the participants as to their preferences, and find out if they have any objections to the way you propose to record what's discussed. If your approach involves drafting meeting minutes or some other sort of report, plan to circulate a draft among the participants to make sure they are OK with it, before you post it on a website or mail it out in final form to all consulting parties. Figuring out your documentation method in advance and adjusting it as consultation begins will save hours over the long haul, especially if the consultation meetings are long and complicated.

CHAPTER 5

Considering

Consultation means the process of... considering... the views of other participants... (36 CFR § 800.16(f))

Clarification: It's Not Sequential

Before going on, let's note something that should be obvious but may be obscured by our chapter organization. When we, and the NHPA Section 106 regulations, say that consultation is *a process of seeking, discussing, and considering the views of other participants, and where feasible seeking agreement with them,* neither we nor the regulations are talking about a rigidly sequential process of "seek-before-you-discuss-before-you-consider-before-you-seek agreement." Yes, the project sponsor or oversight agency does have to "seek" views before they can "discuss" them—unless, of course, someone dumps his views in their lap, or they're otherwise known before anyone starts seeking anything. Both conditions do occur. But whoever is in charge of consultation ought always to be alert to new views and new parties, so in that sense we "seek" views *throughout* the course of any consultation. We don't stop seeking when we start discussing. And "discussing" and "considering" are closely related; we can hardly "discuss" something intelligently without "considering" what's being discussed, and consideration often leads to more discussion, and searching for more ideas and information. "Seeking agreement"—or at least finding and memorializing it—does tend to follow in sequence after seeking, discussing and considering views, but we ought to be looking for ways to agree, and barriers to agreement, from the start. Consultation is a fluid, organic process; we represent it in these chapters as though it were sequential because that's the way the English language works—we string words together in a sequence. The fact

79

Claudia Nissley and Thomas F. King, "Considering" in *Consultation and Cultural Heritage: Let Us Reason Together,* pp. 79-95. © 2014 Left Coast Press, Inc. All rights reserved.

that we say "cats claw and bite" doesn't mean that a cat always claws before it bites. The fact that we say "consultation means seeking views, discussing them, considering them, and seeking agreement," and arrange our chapters accordingly, doesn't mean that consideration can't begin until we're done discussing, or that it can't include seeking agreement. In fact, we may quite reasonably begin "considering" views before we've even solicited them, if, for instance, we already know what someone's concerns are likely to be, or learn about them while doing background research. And "considering," as we'll see, inevitably involves thinking about whether there are grounds for agreement.

That said, what does "considering" the views of other parties entail?

Think About It

Dictionaries generally define "to consider" as "to think carefully" about something, in order to understand or make a decision about it. Duh, you say. Yes, it's obvious, but it follows that if you tell someone that you'll consider her idea or request when you have no intention of thinking about it, you're lying. "Considering" means deliberating, trying the idea on, thinking fairly through its implications, if needed seeking clarification, refining, trying to understand.

In the classes she teaches around the country, Nissley routinely asks her students what they think constitutes good consultation. The answers tend to boil down to being "meaningful"—which in turn means a good-faith, back-and-forth discussion and consideration of people's concerns and what might be done about them. Meaningful consideration is what you ought to give anybody's concerns and ideas; it serves no one's interests to engage in meaningless consideration—an oxymoron if there ever was one.

Considering a Concern

Organic as the whole process may be, considering a concern does have a certain necessary structure. It begins with defining, articulating the concern somehow.

Articulation

A concern may be very clearly articulated: "Neighbors Incensed at Mismanagement of Big Impacts, Inc. (NIMBI) is deeply concerned about the impact of the proposed DeepDark Mine on the Pale Ale Aquifer, whose waters are of great cultural importance to the religious rituals of the Kawako Tribe." But it may very well *not* be so clearly defined, and one of your first jobs may be to figure out just what it is that people are really worrying about.

One thing that may fuzz the clarity of someone's concern is *abstraction*—phrasing a concern in some kind of officialese or other abstract language. Unfortunately, legally grounded environmental impact assessment (EIA) and cultural resource management (CRM) review processes tend to be awash in abstractions—because so are the laws and regulations on which they're based. People who participate in such processes, professionally or otherwise, are virtually forced into communicating in abstract language. Particularly if one doesn't do it for a living, one may not understand such language with precision, and may not use it very well. Conversely, one may resist the government's abstractions and use one's own, which may make little sense to others at the table.

NHPA Section 106, for instance, requires consideration only of project impacts on places included in or eligible for the National Register of Historic Places (NRHP). So if the Kawako Tribe or its NIMBI supporters want their concerns about the Pale Ale Aquifer addressed under that authority, they'll be well advised somehow to describe the aquifer, its water, or the places where the Kawako collect it for their ceremonies in NRHP terms. This will mean referring to specific criteria that were designed mostly with old buildings and archaeological sites in mind (36 CFR § 60.4). The tribe's actual concern about the quality of water in the aquifer may get entirely lost in arguments about the physical integrity of the springs out of which the water gushes, or about whether a spring is best described as a "site," a "district," or maybe a "structure."

Another thing that may get in the way of articulation is *secrecy*. It may be that those Kawako spiritual practices to which the Pale Ale water is so important are very secretive affairs—perhaps because for generations the government forbade them and punished anyone who took part in them, or perhaps because they are thought to be spiritually powerful, not to be dabbled in by or shared with the wrong people.

Felt history can also complicate communication, at least from the perspective of a person who doesn't share the feelings. A member of an indigenous group, for example—and this is *only* an example, because such feelings are by no means experienced only by indigenous people—may automatically relate the current subject of consultation to a long history of the group and its interactions with outsiders. Such a person, particularly if she's a member of a high-context society (see Chapter 3), may spend a great deal of time spelling out this history and its perceived meaning, and only then—*if* then, getting to "the point" as outsiders understand it. By the time she does get to the point, whether verbally or in writing, her interlocutors may be thoroughly confused, turned off, or asleep.

Some things may just be *hard to articulate*, even though (or maybe because) they are integral to a group's identity. Ned Kaufman offers an example:

> *[F]or boys growing up in Brooklyn Heights in the 1950s, neighborhood life revolved around a clutch of stoops that were conducive to the playing of stoop ball; a cul-de-sac where children could ride bicycles without fear of traffic was another important spot, as was a playground at which the Good Humor truck stopped (and continues to stop)* (Kaufman 2009:47-48).

Kaufman argues that such "story sites" are vital parts of a neighborhood's identity, and that their existence fosters citizenship and conserves social capital—critical to maintaining a livable, functioning community. But how would a Brooklyn Heights resident articulate his feeling that stoops (small porches) or a bike-friendly cul-de-sac are important enough to be considered when changes are planned to the neighborhood? How could he make his feelings known without seeming silly to himself and others?

So if you're trying to consider someone's views, or make sure others do so, one of your first tasks may be to help people articulate their views in ways that you and others can understand and respect. This may be a delicate matter, particularly if secrecy or a group's particular communication style is among the things standing in the way. Exactly how you do it depends on the situation—who's involved, what they're concerned about, what stands in the way of articulating it. But it will help to remember the Golden Rule: if you were trying to talk or write about something meaningful to you, to someone with a background very different from yours, how would you want to be treated by that someone? What kind of help would you appreciate in making your concern known?

Of course, if you're working for the project sponsor you may want to say: "This isn't my problem. If the Kawako or the NIMBI's or stooped people in

Brooklyn Heights can't articulate their concerns in a way that makes sense to me and my clients or superiors, or lawyers, that's *their* problem." That's understandable, and if you see your job as being to advance the project through whatever environmental and cultural reviews are required with minimum muss and fuss, you may write the Kawako a dismissive letter or compose an obscure response paragraph in your impact assessment, and get on with it. But if you think your job is to resolve objections to the project, or arrive at a balanced decision about it in the public interest, then you need to try to do more. And dismissive responses can come back to haunt you. The tribe or the NIMBIs or the Brooklyn Heights ball-players may find themselves a good lawyer or a sympathetic legislator, and being forced to consider their concerns late in project planning may be a lot less comfortable than doing so on your own, at the outset.

How Does the Concern Relate?

As you begin to understand what the concern is, you can begin to figure out how it relates to the project at hand and the decision to be made. This, too, may not be intuitively obvious. If you're reviewing plans for the DeepDark Mine under NHPA Section 106, for instance, it may be something of a stretch to understand how Kawako religious practices and the quality of water in the Pale Ale Aquifer relate to impacts on historic places. It may be especially hard if you're accustomed to thinking of historic places as old architecture or archaeological sites. But think it through; ask yourself questions. In this case,

Question: Districts, sites, buildings, structures, and objects can be eligible for the NRHP. Could any such things be involved in the Kawako case?

Answer: Well, maybe the springs from which the Kawako get their water are eligible sites, or landscapes/districts (your answer, of course, may differ).

Question: Section 106 review is about resolving adverse effects on NRHP-eligible places. Could polluting the aquifer that feeds the springs constitute an adverse effect on them from a historic preservation point of view?

Answer: If the water in the NRHP-eligible springs becomes unusable for the cultural/ritual purposes that make the springs eligible, then that's certainly—in the words of the Section 106 regulations—an alteration to "the characteristics of a historic property that qualify the property for inclusion in the National Register in a manner that would diminish the integrity of the property's location, design, setting, materials, workmanship, feeling, or association" (36 CFR § 800.5(a)(1)). This was essentially the reason that the U.S. Navy's plans for geothermal power generation near Coso Hot Springs in California came under Section 106 review back in the 1980s—because the springs were eligible for the NRHP based on their significance to local tribes, and the geothermal development might alter the volume or character of their flow (King 2003:185).

So yes, in this case, with reference to NHPA Section 106, the Kawako concern about water quality does qualify for consideration. Of course, it may very well qualify for consideration under other laws as well—in this case the National Environmental Policy Act, the American Indian Religious Freedom Act, the Religious Freedom Restoration Act, and maybe the Clean Water Act. In another country, a whole range of different laws might apply—or not.

Depending on your point of view, you can approach a question like this either with the intent of finding a way to relate the concern to the legal framework with which you're working, or with the intent of not finding such a way, and even of impeding anyone else's efforts to find one. We recommend that you do the former—look for ways to relate people's concerns to the laws and regulations under which you're working—not only because we think it's the right thing to do, but because if you do, you may be on your way to bringing the concerned people around to agreement on your project. Remember Queen Elizabeth's second "dead good reason" for consultation.

On the other hand, if you try to avoid relating a concern to the legal system under which your project is being reviewed, you're leaving it hanging out there in limbo, to fester and grow worse. Our advice would be to find a way to make the concern relate to some sort of process through which you can try to address and resolve it.

If you're representing the Kawako, or NIMBI, or the people of Brooklyn Heights, it will help you if you try to get a bit familiar with the laws, regulations, and abstractions with which the project sponsor and oversight agencies are dealing. At the very least, don't accept the sponsor's or an agency's experts as the last word on how to interpret, say, the NRHP criteria. Insist that they explain themselves, and if you can, consult your own experts. If you're dealing with U.S. "cultural resource" laws, at least check out King 2007 and/or 2013.

It's unfortunate, we think, that we have to go through a nit-picking, hair-splitting exercise in applying things like NRHP Section 106 adverse effect criteria in order to address someone's concerns. As we said earlier, we think getting wrapped up in abstractions like these can complicate communication and thus may get in the way of resolving concerns. But in every legal regime we know of, something of this kind has to be done, if that legal system requires that any consideration at all be given to subjective cultural values in the environment.

What Can We Do About It?

Having recognized a concern and figured out how it relates to the laws, regulations, and procedures under which we're working, we can think about how to deal with it. What options are open to us to address the concern, resolve the problem?

There almost always *are* options, if you look for them with an open, creative mind. There are some habits of thought that get in the way of applying creativity to solution-seeking, however, so here are a few cautionary notes.

Rote "Solutions" Particularly if you've been in your job for awhile, and have dealt with multiple projects—or if you're relying on experienced experts in fields like historic preservation or heritage studies—you'll need to be alert to the danger of opting automatically for rote solutions to the problem, whatever it is.

For instance, for many historic preservation practitioners in the United States today, there are two standard solutions to almost any problem involving historic buildings, structures, and designed landscapes.

1. Rehabilitate them following the *Secretary of the Interior's Standards for Rehabilitation;* and/or

2. Document them following the standards of the Historic American Buildings Survey (HABS), Historic American Engineering Record (HAER), or Historic American Landscapes Survey (HALS),[1] and then (implicitly) demolish them.

These are perfectly good solutions to some problems, sometimes, but often they're quite irrelevant, and more often they need some creative tweaking in order to make them useful. For example, it may be that the interior of a building is insignificant or so thoroughly altered that it doesn't matter what changes are made to it, and the *Secretary of the Interior's Standards* are relevant only to making changes in the exterior—or vice-versa. And HABS/HAER/HALS documentation methods are not the only methods available, if documentation is appropriate at all. For example, consider cellphone applications with which you can load and access historical views of a place[2]— a far more accessible, perhaps less expensive, and more engaging means of documentation than the preparation of static measured drawings or even videos. In some cases, too, documentation simply serves no purpose; it is proposed only because it is thought to be the standard thing to do.

King once worked on a case in which a private developer, scheduled to bring some ten million dollars in private capital into the adaptive use of a surplus historic military base, utterly refused to be bound by the *Secretary's Standards for Rehabilitation*, so irritated was he at the nit-picking way the standards had been interpreted in their application to a previous project. He'd walk away from the project, he said, if he was required to follow the standards. By simply stipulating that the *Standards* would be used as *non-binding guidelines*, to the extent it was cost-effective to do so, we kept the developer in the project and—because the *Standards* in fact are pretty commonsensical, and tend to be cost-effective—got a very successful, attractive rehab project that was entirely sensitive to the character of the historic buildings. Similarly, Nissley was involved in the construction of a new entrance to the Denver Mint, whose ongoing functions dictated that security needs had to trump historic aesthetics. A diverse group of consulting parties wound up working closely with the architects designing the project to develop an approach that reflected but did not adhere strictly to the *Standards*, producing an entrance that met the Mint's security needs while respecting the building's character.

Archaeological data recovery—aka salvage or rescue archaeology—is another rote "solution" to conflicts between development and sites that contain information on history or prehistory. Again, it may be a perfectly good solution, but it very likely will not "solve" the conflict between development and the interests of people who feel a cultural or spiritual connection with those who lived, worshipped, or buried their dead at such sites. Opting for data recovery may even exacerbate the conflict: "You're not only proposing to bulldoze our ancestors' graves; you want to give their contents to the archaeologists to fondle!"

When the U.S. General Services Administration (GSA) in the 1990s learned from old maps that there was an eighteenth century "Negro Burial Ground" on the site of its proposed office building in New York City, its officials automatically assumed that archaeological data recovery would take care of the conflict. Bad move. African-American communities and others around the world protested what they saw as GSA's callous treatment of the enslaved ancestors, taking their complaints to the U.S. Congress. The project had to be delayed and redesigned at a cost of somewhere around US$100 million (Hansen & McGowan 1998; McCarthy 1996, 2008).

It's not only ancestral graves that may be poor subjects for data recovery. As we're writing this book there's a controversy over the Sarpy Creek Bison Kill site on the Crow reservation in Montana. A site where bison were butchered some 2,000 years ago, Sarpy Creek was in the way of a proposed coal mine, and the method chosen to deal with this conflict was archaeological data recovery using heavy equipment, coupled with some kind of "monitoring".[3] Unfortunately, the selection was apparently made without consulting all the concerned parties, including Crow tribal interests who regard the site as a place of spiritual power and archaeologists who say they would—if they'd had the chance—have argued for "in place" preservation or a more careful, detailed excavation than was performed. At last report in late 2012 the mine was on hold and some tribal officials responsible for the decision had lost their jobs (MacMillan 2012).

Abstractions Again   Laws and regulations tend to insist—without ever exactly saying so—that we couch our problems and solutions in abstract terms. This may be inevitable, but for the same reasons discussed earlier with respect to articulating concerns, it can impede communication and frustrate efforts to resolve them.

In the NHPA Section 106 regulations, for instance, a project has an adverse effect on a historic place if it may somehow diminish the "integrity" of those qualities that make the place eligible for the NRHP. Never mind how badly it messes the place up in the eyes of those who love it; what often becomes the subject of debate among specialists is whether it diminishes the quality of the abstraction: "eligibility for the NRHP." That eligibility, of course, is typically assessed by professionals in history, archaeology, and other scholarly fields with reference to the general-purpose criteria set forth in the NRHP regulations (36 CFR § 60.4).

Specialists in historic preservation—like us—can debate endlessly about such abstractions, and we tend to enjoy it. It's kind of like Sudoku, or working out a crossword puzzle. This can be maddening to people who are just trying to get consideration for a place they love, and it can be equally maddening to people who want to get on with a project that may affect that place. We ought to try to respect the concerns of both kinds of people—and others, of course—and not reduce review of a project to a debate about abstractions meaningful only to us.

We can get so wrapped up in our abstractions that we come to think that they dictate how something will be treated. Many agencies and consultants, for example, have decided that if they and a State Historic Preservation Officer (SHPO) find that a place is eligible for the NRHP only under "Criterion D" for its probable possession of significant information about the past,[4] then it is automatically OK to resolve any potential adverse effect on it through archaeological data recovery or even "monitoring." That's not what any regulation says, but it's where abstractions lead us: if it's a D place we can dig it up and say it's been preserved, while if it's an A place, a B place, or a C place, we can't. So we're sorry, Ms. Green, but we've determined that your grandma's homestead is eligible for the NRHP under criterion D, so we're allowed to dig it up and then destroy it. The fact that this makes your eyes glaze over or fill with tears doesn't matter.

Try to remember: we're not going through all this review and consultation to please the god of abstract concepts; we're trying to resolve real conflicts between real people.

Staying in your Comfort Zone   "I'm not comfortable with that," has become a common modern (or post-modern) conversation-killer, often bringing discussion of a topic to a screeching stop. In practice, under laws like NHPA Section 106, it's often used by people in authority, such as SHPO staff, to kill discussion of things that they don't understand to be "preservation solutions." This in turn usually means ideas or practices with which the speaker is not familiar and doesn't want to become familiar.

In most U.S. states, for instance, historic and prehistoric artifacts found on private land belong to the private landowners. Many archaeologists are not comfortable with this fact, so in a consultation where the disposition of artifacts is an issue, they prefer not to discuss the implications of private ownership—

which naturally include the possibility of sale or discard. So the issue simply doesn't get addressed, and who knows what happens to the artifacts? If it *were* addressed, the options addressed might include sale to museums, sale to private parties with provision for access should the need to examine them arise, and intensive documentation before sale. But if you're an archaeologist, discussing such matters may make you squirm, so you ignore them.

With respect, what makes you squirm is not relevant. Sure, we shouldn't make anyone squirm unnecessarily, but the mere fact that someone is made uncomfortable—particularly someone like a government employee or contractor who's being paid to advise—is no excuse for excluding a concern or a solution from consideration.

Illegalities and Immoralities   Someone may propose a solution that you or others find morally or ethically offensive, or even flatly illegal. In such a case the temptation may be to reject the solution out of hand—to not consider it. This may be a mistake. For one thing others may not share your ethics, your morality, and even if you firmly believe that they were given you by the hand or voice of God, you can't force others to buy into them. As for legalities—no, in the end you can't agree to something that's illegal, but that doesn't mean you can't or shouldn't consider it. By considering it you may come to understand what interests seem—to whoever's proposing it—to justify the illegal proposition, and then you can explore *legal* ways to address those interests.

In a number of cases we've both been involved in, tribal or local interests have said that if the government absolutely insists on destroying something of great cultural, even spiritual importance to them, then government ought to pay for cultural programming on radio or television, or sponsor a website, or buy land for the tribe or community to use for cultural purposes, or fund a cultural center, or just cough up X number of dollars. We used to have a colleague who got absolutely livid at such proposals, calling them extortion. From his perspective—which we could entirely understand—they *were* extortionate, and sometimes they seemed that way to us, too. But from the point of view of the tribe or community, they might make perfect sense: "You're contributing to the erosion of our culture; you can make up for that by giving us the money we need to shore it up." There's no question that you have to be careful with such proposals, and think about how they may be perceived, but it's unreasonable to turn them down without consideration simply because they offend or trouble you.

Years ago, King worked on a case in Micronesia involving construction of an airport on an island's fringing reef, offshore from a traditional village (Parker & King 1987). An issue that arose during the negotiation of an MOA under NHPA Section 106 was access to the reef margin by the villagers. Why did they need access to the reef margin? Well, for several reasons, but the most urgent was that the village had no sewerage facilities, so people visited the reef margin to relieve their bladders and bowels. Some of the government's negotiators were appalled: "We can't consider that," they cried. "Pooping on the reef is against the law!" "Well," said the village chief, "then in the alternative, perhaps the government could buy all my people lifetime supplies of corks." In the end (as it were), the government found a way to accelerate construction of a sewer to serve the village, and in the interim quietly left an unlocked gate in the airport perimeter fence.

Just as a solution that may seem immoral or unethical to you may seem perfectly fine to another consulting party, a solution that seems fine to you may outrage others. Nissley, as Wyoming State Historic Preservation Officer, was involved in consultation on a proposed coal mine in which the project sponsor, spurred by the need to get a permit within the next three months, simply offered money to several Indian tribes to compensate for taking a ridge covered with stone alignments that the tribes regarded as sacred. The company's offer was quite low, and the state permitting agency proposed that it should be doubled. Both missed the indignant reactions of the tribal representatives to their commodification of the tribes' heritage.

It's important to remember that your values, ethics, and morals, and even your interpretations of law, are not necessarily shared by all the consulting parties. An idea may offend you, but that doesn't necessarily make it wrong. Conversely, what seems like a perfectly reasonable, legal, moral and righteous solution to you may be deeply offensive to others, and even proposing it may derail the consultation.

Addressing Alternatives

Considering concerns about a project inevitably involves considering alternatives—alternatives to the project overall, and alternatives to particular elements or aspects of the project. Lawyers we've dealt with on some NHPA Section 106 cases have argued that their clients don't need to consider alternatives because Section 106 doesn't explicitly require it; only the National Environmental Policy Act (NEPA) does so. It's this kind of mindless hair-splitting that justifies the solution proposed by Shakespeare's Dick the Butcher: "let's kill all the lawyers."[5]

Decision making, and the consideration leading to it, *always* involves considering alternatives. Should you get up at six in the morning, or exercise the alternative of staying in bed? Should you have a beer, or exercise the alternative of restraint, or of having a straight shot of Scotch?

The NEPA regulations of the Council on Environmental Quality (CEQ) provide a list of "mitigation measures" that constitutes a pretty good roster of alternatives that ought to be considered:

(a) Avoiding the impact altogether by not taking a certain action or parts of an action.

(b) Minimizing impacts by limiting the degree or magnitude of the action and its implementation.

(c) Rectifying the impact by repairing, rehabilitating, or restoring the affected environment.

(d) Reducing or eliminating the impact over time by preservation and maintenance operations during the life of the action.

(e) Compensating for the impact by replacing or providing substitute resources or environments.

(40 CFR § 1508.20)

The first and last items merit special attention. "Not taking" an action obviously means either giving up a project purpose altogether or seeking some alternative means of achieving its purpose. If the project is to put in wind turbines to pump 250 megawatts of electricity into the southeast Utazona power grid, and lots of objections are arising to the project, what alternative ways are there to generate those 250 MW? How about rooftop solar arrays? How about increasing the output of the nearby hydropower facility? What about energy conservation? Or is it this project or no power? The answer will vary from case to case, but this is a kind of question that often must be pursued, no matter what legal authority drives the project review.

As for the last item, "compensation" can take many forms. The iconic method of "compensatory mitigation," developed in the U.S. in the context of NEPA and Clean Water Act compliance, involves the creation of wetlands to compensate for wetlands filled. Similar compensations can be considered when we're dealing with cultural resource/heritage issues. Land may be purchased and added to an Indian tribe's reservation, in compensation for loss of ancestral sites. Funding may be provided to a local museum to compensate for the loss of historic places. A revolving fund may be created to support local historic preservation efforts, in compensation for knocking down some historic buildings.

Information Needs

Considering people's concerns and alternatives may reveal the need to share information that you hadn't planned to share, or to develop new information. The court in *Pueblo of Sandia* criticized the Forest Service for, among other things, not sharing information that a consulting party (in that case the SHPO) needed to participate properly in review.[6] A similar criticism was a key factor in *Comanche Nation v. United States*, where the court found that details about the proposed project (a warehouse that would impede views of a spiritual site) had been buried in lengthy attachments to environmental documents, where the tribe could not find them without extensive research.[7]

The Golden Rule Again

The Golden Rule is a good guide when you're thinking about what information to share with consulting parties. What kind of information would *you* want, if you were in the consulting parties' positions, and in what form would you want it? That's what you ought to supply them, and don't hide it among multiple other documents, or in obscure appendices to planning papers.

Of course, if they ask for something different from what you can imagine yourself asking for, or you're pretty sure that they need something else, you ought to supply that, too. For example, if an issue circulates around an interpretation of law, and you have access to a good law library and a consulting party doesn't, it's only courteous to send them a copy of whatever law, regulation, court decision, or legal opinion you think is relevant.

Which brings us to another point…

Know What You're Talking About

In our (Nissley's and King's) business, where we often are called upon to help multiple consulting parties consider one another's points of view and seek agreement, we often find people making very confident statements about "the law," "the regulations," or some other foundational authority. Their statements are very confident, but often dead wrong, or at least ignorant of the law's or regulations' nuances. Any time you're tempted to share this kind of information—your interpretation, or your agency's or client's, about what's required, dictated, defined or encouraged by some authoritative document—for heaven's sake *read the document*! Make sure you understand it, and that your interpretation of it is, if not demonstrably correct, at least arguably on-point. We regularly find ourselves trying to walk consulting parties (including our clients) back from irresoluble conflicts grounded in myths about what laws and regulations require. You should always question authoritative statements about what "the law" requires—particularly if those statements are your own.

Doing Studies

If you're the project proponent or responsible agency, you may need to do new studies, or direct that they're done, to address issues that come up during consultation. For instance, if rooftop solar arrays are brought up as an alternative to your client's wind power project, and that alternative hasn't already been reasonably considered, it may be necessary to look into it, to find out whether it's a viable way to achieve the project's purpose. The temptation will be not to "waste" the time and money on doing such studies. You, your agency, or your client may be utterly convinced that the alternative won't work, or have no interest in pursuing it even if it would. But considering alternatives is at the heart of good faith consultation, and you can't consider alternatives without understanding what they are, and what their implications may be.

King and a colleague were recently involved in a proposal to demolish a historic building to put in a new facility on a federal installation. The old building, we were told, had to go; there was no place else to put in the new facility. Visiting the site after reading the installation's long-term development plan, we asked: "Why can't the new building go over there, on that patch of trashed-up vacant land, and then why can't you rehabilitate the historic building to meet this other need that's laid out in your development plan?" We might well have been told to shut our traps, draw our consulting fees and go away had the SHPO not backed us up, but when she did, the clients tasked their architect/engineer firm to study the alternative. They found that it would not only work, but would save the government a bit of money in the process. The study done by the architect/engineer wasn't very costly, and it took a lot less time than the clients might have spent in a vituperative argument over demolition.

These things do happen. Your agency's or client's preferred alternative may not really be the best way to solve whatever problem it's aimed at. Others may have good ideas, and these may be very much worth the investment of time and money to study—not only to demonstrate to some skeptical oversight agency or judge that you've consulted in good faith, but because sometimes those who question the preferred alternative have a better one to suggest.

Documenting Consideration

Because you *may* have to demonstrate to a skeptical overseeing body or court of law that you've done what the laws and regulations require, and for your own future reference, you should try to document whatever you do to consider the views of consulting parties. This record is almost inevitably going to be messy, including emails, telephone logs, copies of letters, reports on studies, and so on, but the more organized you can make it, the better. Your agency or company may have pre-established ways of keeping records; if so, you obviously ought to use them, but also make sure they aren't unduly limiting. You may need to keep things that your records management system doesn't require or even allow you to keep, and in such a case you need to find a way to adjust or work around the system.

Among U.S. federal agencies, records must be kept in ways that are consistent with regulations issued under the Federal Records Act (FRA). FRA regulations, and the agency procedures they spawn, tend to be pretty complicated and are, unfortunately, often honored in the breach. Here again you need to learn what the pertinent regulations and procedures actually say, and try to make your recordkeeping consistent. At the same time, if the FRA procedures that apply to you don't look like they'll give you a useful, consultable record of what's been proposed and how you've considered it, you need to explore going beyond what the procedures require, or flexing them somehow. The NHPA Section 106 regulations provide some useful advice about documentation, requiring that any "determination, finding, or agreement" be "supported by sufficient documentation to enable any reviewing parties to understand its basis,"[8] including "copies or summaries of any views provided by consulting parties and the public."[7]

A useful rule of thumb is to imagine yourself, ten or twenty years from now, being asked by a court how a given issue was considered. You (or your successor) should be able to answer, and dig up the documents that support the answer.

CHAPTER 6

Seeking Agreement

Consultation means the process of seeking, discussing, and considering the views of other participants, and, where feasible, seeking agreement with them... (36 CFR § 800.16(f))

"Where Feasible"

Let's begin with those two pesky words in the NHPA Section 106 regulations: "where feasible."

They may have to be there, though we think they could have been left out without affecting the meaning of the sentence. It is certainly a fact that agreement can't always be reached, and sometimes may not be necessary, desirable, or worth pursuing. We have been involved in NHPA Section 106 cases recently in which the issues involved were so minor, and the points of disagreement so technical, that it hardly seemed necessary or useful to dignify them by trying to reach and memorialize an agreement. Even in such cases, the structure of the Section 106 regulations has given us no choice but to seek formal, documented agreements, because that's what they require when an "adverse effect" is found on a historic property. Where one isn't bound by such regulations, it seems foolish to seek agreement just for agreement's sake. "Where feasible" provides some wiggle room.

On the other hand, those two little words can give agencies and project sponsors room to wiggle out of consultation altogether. Is it "not appropriate" to seek agreement about anything but technical hair-splits? Is it "not appropriate" if the project sponsor just doesn't have the time or inclination? If it just seems like too much trouble? If you don't like the people who want to

96

Claudia Nissley and Thomas F. King, "Seeking Agreement" in *Consultation and Cultural Heritage: Let Us Reason Together,* pp. 96-119. © 2014 Left Coast Press, Inc. All rights reserved.

consult? If you don't think there's an absolute legal requirement to hear what they have to say? And if it's not "appropriate" to seek agreement, then what's the point in consulting at all, and how meaningful can that consultation be?

And there are solid substantive reasons for trying to reach and memorialize an agreement, even on relatively minor and non-controversial matters. A written agreement can encapsulate what everybody thinks about a project's effects and how to handle them, so if uncertainties arise down the road, or new people get involved, or plans change, there's an understood baseline from which to make any necessary adjustments.

Let's not beat around the bush: in our view it is *always* "appropriate" to seek agreement, through good-faith consultation, where there's an issue that people care about. The mere fact that it's inconvenient, or uncomfortable, or requires you to deal with people you, your agency, or your client would rather ignore does not make seeking agreement inappropriate. Nor is it inappropriate just because there's no specific law, regulation, or national policy saying you *must* try to agree. On the other hand, it's too bad that some regulations force us through the hassle of developing elaborate formal agreements where there's no substantive issue to resolve.

Negotiation: In Consultation and Versus Consultation

We in the CRM/EIA worlds often uses the words "consultation" and "negotiation" as though they were synonyms, but they're not, and we ought to be clear about this (see Nissley 2011:444-5, 450-51). Negotiation can be a *part* of consultation, and particularly at the stage of seeking agreement any good consultation at least closely resembles negotiation, but the two terms mean different things, and it's important to understand the distinction.

Negotiation is aimed at some agreed-upon outcome. We typically seek to negotiate an agreement about what to do—for instance, how to mitigate the impact of a project on some aspect of the environment. Moreover, use of the term carries with it some implication that all sides have the power to influence the outcome. Power may not be balanced—one side may have a lot more of it than others, but none of the negotiators is completely without it.

Consultation does not necessarily have agreement as its intended outcome. It may have—or be perceived by some of its participants to have—a rather passive purpose, such as seeking or conveying information or building understanding.

Quite often, too, the party responsible for consulting others has all or most of the power, while those being consulted have little or none.

Of course, there are different kinds of power, which can be used in many ways to balance the consultative equation. For instance:

1. In consultation between the United States government and a federally recognized Indian tribe, the federal government has virtually all the explicit, formal power; in the end it can do what it wishes, after consulting a tribal government about it—which the U.S. government may take to mean only informing the tribe, listening to tribal views, and maybe considering such views to the extent it's convenient. But the tribe has a degree of power flowing from the fiduciary "trust" relationship the U.S. government supposedly has toward it, and in some cases from specific or general treaty rights. The tribe—even when not a federally recognized one—may also be able to exercise moral, ethical, psychological, and hence political power, based on the history of its oppression over the years. It may be able to generate public sympathy based on its history and culture, and draw on formal statements of policy like the United Nations Declaration on the Rights of Indigenous People (see Fuller 2011:375-81) and federal guidelines about avoiding environmental injustice. It may have the legal expertise and financial resources to take the government to court. All this may make it difficult for the U.S. government to ignore the tribe's concerns; the government may be forced to negotiate.

2. In consultation under NHPA Section 106, the U.S. government is entirely in the driver's seat, but must (in theory) follow the rules of the road set forth in the Section 106 regulations. As we know, these regulations define "consultation" to include "where feasible, seeking agreement" with the State Historic Preservation Officer, Indian tribes, and other parties. So—again in theory—an agency cannot "consult" under Section 106 merely by telling consulting parties what it plans to do, listening to their complaints, and ignoring them; it must seek agreement, whether it reaches it or not. This means that there must be some give and take among the parties; for all intents and purposes they must negotiate—unless, of course, the government determines for some reason that seeking agreement is not "feasible." Moreover, the regulations allow some consulting parties—admittedly, most explicitly only the State or Tribal Historic Preservation Officer (SHPO/THPO)—to push con-

sultation to higher levels in the regulatory system, or even terminate it and force an agency to seek Advisory Council comment, which can be embarrassing for the agency responsible. This gives consulting parties a degree of power to force the government into actual negotiation.

However attractive it may be to a government agency to consult by simply informing, getting input, and ignoring it as it proceeds with its project, agencies are usually better advised to create at least the impression of negotiating, especially when consulting with the SHPO/THPO and tribes under NHPA Section 106. When doing environmental impact assessment (EIA) under the National Environmental Policy Act (NEPA), an agency has more leeway to do only "I-cubed consultation"—inform, get input, and ignore.[1] It has to pretend not to ignore the input—it has to document some sort of response—but there is little practical requirement that the response be meaningful (see King 2009:127-40).

Non-governmental consulting parties need to go into consultation with eyes wide open, knowing that the government probably does not define the term as synonymous with negotiation, and recognizing that they have little or no explicit power to make the consultation negotiative. A non-governmental party needs to think through what it may do to garner more power—to convince the (ir)responsible agency that it's in its interests to negotiate. You may never have to use this power explicitly, but having it, and letting the agency or sponsor know you have it, can be invaluable.

There are many ways to balance the government's power, or at least to try to do so. For instance:

1. By knowing relevant legal requirements and deploying that knowledge, thus raising the specter of endless litigation (particularly if you can also deploy a good lawyer or two);

2. By building alliances with others having more explicit power (in the U.S., federally recognized Indian tribes and State Historic Preservation Officers, for example);

3. By building bridges to the news media and preparing to burden the agency and sponsor with adverse publicity; and

4. By gaining the support of political actors (such as, in the U.S., members of congress) who can question the agency, demand answers, and get them.

No one should go into consultation with any agency of any government trusting the agency to negotiate in good faith toward a mutually agreeable outcome. The agency's intention is almost always to do whatever it has decided or been directed to do, and however much it may "consult"—in the sense of having meetings, writing letters, and sharing paperwork—it will *negotiate* only to the extent it is required to by law or impelled to by fear, repeated exposure to public outrage, or recurrent frustration in its effort to have its way. Nicholas Dorochoff (2007) provides useful guidance in how to prevail on others to negotiate, and how to carry out a negotiation.

Agreement is Always Optional

Everyone should also be clear about the fact that in most cases where environmental and/or historic preservation laws are the drivers of consultation, reaching agreement is not mandatory. Under NHPA Section 106, for instance, once an agency has initiated consultation, and made some effort to carry it forward (the rules are ill-defined for how serious that effort must be), it can terminate consultation, get the final comments of the Advisory Council on Historic Preservation (ACHP), and then make its decision, whatever that decision may be. Playing the termination card is not risk-free for the agency: the ACHP comment goes to the very top dog in the agency, who must give it her personal attention. Nobody on the lower rungs of an agency's career ladder welcomes scrutiny from the top, unless they're doing something that will merit pats on the back. That said, however, the termination option is always there as an agency's alternative to negotiation.

Consultation under Section 7 of the U.S. Endangered Species Act—an interagency affair involving only the agency responsible for the action and either the Fish and Wildlife Service (FWS) or the National Marine Fisheries Service (NMFS)—doesn't exactly lead to negotiating an agreement but to a "Biological Opinion" rendered by FWS or NMFS, which an agency can't ignore but doesn't entirely have to adhere to either. Other environmental and cultural resource laws, to the extent they require consultation at all, are even less demanding in terms of agreement. Still, though, a documented agreement is the surest way of demonstrating that you've satisfied someone's concern about your project, so it's worth working toward if you're a project sponsor. It's also usually worth trying for an agreement if you represent an outside party who wants the sponsor—or better, a theoretically objective oversight agency—to address your concerns. Just don't kid yourself into thinking that the agency or sponsor *must* reach agreement with you. Unless you have a special card up your sleeve, like the terms of a treaty negotiated centuries ago by your prescient tribal ancestors, the agency in the end can call off the game and walk away with the chips.

Working Toward Agreement

With that dour warning behind us, let's assume it's in everybody's interests to work toward an agreement. How do we do it? Of course, there are lots of routes to agreement—or to disagreement—but here are some essential guidelines.

Don't Write it First

This is a terribly common mistake in NHPA Section 106 consultation. You know what you want the agreement to say, so—particularly if you're working for the responsible agency or project sponsor—you're tempted to draft the agreement and start the consultation by laying it before the consulting parties to sign. We've seen agencies and project sponsors forget about consultation altogether and try to contract with consultants to write agreements without talking to *anybody*. This is crazy—except in those cases (all too common in practice under NHPA Section 106) where there's really no disagreement, and the only reason for a documented agreement is to satisfy the regulations.

Assuming we're dealing with a case in which there *is* disagreement, apply the Golden Rule. How would you like it if someone slapped down a piece of paper in front of you at the beginning of a discussion about something important to you, and said: "Here's our agreement, whaddya think?" Insulted? Patronized? Like the deck was stacked against you? You bet. Too-early agreement-drafting can be a consultation killer. If you're interested in serious consultation, you won't do it.

The other reason to avoid early drafting goes back to Queen Elizabeth's first rationale for consultation—learning things you hadn't considered. Any "agreement" you draft in your own closet or cubicle, or within your own team, without input from other consulting parties, is going to be limited by your own perspectives, your own priorities, and your own information. You may miss a solution that will work best for everyone.

The same arguments apply to making bilateral deals in a consultation that ought to be multilateral. This happens a good deal under NHPA Section 106, because an agency is required to consult with the SHPO[2] but has discretion about who else it consults, and because agencies tend to assume that SHPOs are "the experts" when it comes to historic preservation. The NHPA Section 106 regulations even say—with no stated rationale whatever—that the SHPO "reflects the interests of the State and its citizens in the preservation of their cultural heritage" (36 CFR § 800.2(c)(1)(i)). So agencies are tempted to draft agreements only with them and expect everybody else to go along—assuming they've even let others into the party. This bilateralism can be just as infuriating to another consulting party as unilateral agreement drafting, and can destroy any impression of even-handedness the SHPO may want to maintain. Moreover, it can preclude consideration of viable alternatives. SHPOs are no more infallible or all-knowing than federal agencies or project sponsors.

All that said, there are occasions when drafting an agreement up-front can be a useful strategy for a party *other than the sponsor or oversight agency* to employ. Laying out your proposal before the sponsor or agency has a chance to articulate its own can give you a leg up in the negotiations—the other side has to critique your proposal, rather than leaving you to critique theirs. This assumes, of course, that you have something to propose other than "abandon this project and go away."

Try Out Solutions

While you shouldn't lay a fully fleshed out agreement in front of everyone (unless it's strategic to do so), it may be very helpful to capture possible solutions that have been advanced, or even just implied, in the course of consultation. This can help focus everyone's attention on a range of options, and facilitate communication. For instance, if you're managing or facilitating a consultation, you might write, email, or just say something like this to one or more of the consulting parties:

> On February 31st the DeepDark Mining Company gave us all a
> technical proposal outlining how it believes it can put in the mine
> without polluting the PaleAle Aquifer. What's your reaction to this
> proposal? If you don't like it, can you suggest other options besides

the "no action" alternative—with the understanding that the "no action" alternative is also on the table for discussion?

Sometimes an alternative or concern may not be explicitly proposed; it may be implied, hiding out in the thicket of words produced by the consultation, waiting to be noticed. It may be productive to try to flush it out—for instance, by asking a participant something like this:

> During our February 31st meeting, you seemed to us to imply that there might be a way to compensate for possible impacts on the PaleAle Aquifer. If you think that's the case, can you elaborate a bit?

And don't be too shy about offering your own ideas, provided you're reasonably sure you can phrase them in ways that won't drive others out of the negotiation, or crazy. King once proposed mitigating impacts on a Micronesian village's access to natural food sources on its reef by financing the purchase of a pig for every resident family—pork being a staple of the local diet. The idea was laughed off the table, but laughter was all it provoked. Had the village been ruled by the militant Islamists, Nissley would probably be authoring this book by herself.

The other parties laughed, too, when during consultation on the transfer of Midway Atoll in the Pacific from the U.S. Navy to the Fish and Wildlife Service, Nissley proposed preserving its vacant historic buildings for potential use to accommodate ecotourism—a new phenomenon at the time. The agencies involved in consultation thought the atoll far too remote to attract such use. Eventually, though, they signed an agreement including Nissley's proposal among others, and in the decades since, the buildings have experienced a high rate of use by ecotourists and wildlife researchers alike.

Laying out possible options early in a negotiation is not without its downside. It can tempt everyone to focus *only* on a single range of options, and that's something to guard against. You should at least encourage people not to be limited by the solutions you've laid out, or not lay them out at all until everyone has had a chance to offer their own ideas—to which you ought to listen, carefully and with an open mind.

Be Alert to and Allow for Cultural Differences

As the example of King's pigs suggests, it's important to keep the cultural values of your consulting partners in mind. Culture may prevent some things from being discussed, or it may define ways in which they *can* be discussed, or when and where they can be discussed. It may be unwise to plan meetings in the building where your consulting partner's ancestors were imprisoned and tortured during some past period of strife—or are thought to have been, regardless of the "reality" of that belief in your eyes or the eyes of others. It may be quite infeasible to negotiate, or to carry on a particular kind of negotiation, during a particular season of the year, around the time of a religious festival or holy day, or at least scheduling may affect the quality of the discussion. If your negotiating partners are Muslim and it's Ramadan, expect them to be a bit hungry and cranky, especially in the afternoon. And some traditional groups, like it or not, don't want to negotiate with women, or with men, or with people of differing religious or sexual persuasions. It can be very tricky to accommodate these biases, and indeed your own predilections, or the law, may demand that you *not* accommodate them, but you'd be ill-advised not to acknowledge that they may exist, and that they may affect your negotiation.

Culture also helps define the issues that people think need to be addressed in an agreement, and the solutions they find attractive. These issues and solutions may be surprising to someone whose culture is that of the "mainstream." For example, consider the different ranges of solutions that may seem appropriate to "low context" and "high context" negotiators.

In Chapter 3 we touched on Edward Hall's (1976) classification of communication styles along a continuum from "low context" to "high context." We also mentioned Raymond Cohen's (1997) book about how the context-based styles of negotiation have influenced international diplomacy. You'll recall that most Anglo-Americans—and others whose sociocultural backgrounds lie in Great Britain or western Europe—are relatively low context communicators, talking and writing mostly to share information. Virtually everyone else in the world is a higher-context communicator. For them, communication is not primarily about transferring information but about expressing, honoring, maintaining, or changing social expectations and status relationships, and about maintaining, gaining, or losing face. While a low-context communicator may be mostly or entirely concerned about sharing ideas with the other parties to the conversation, the high-context communicator may be at least as worried about how his words will be interpreted by a range of other people and groups, some or all of whom may not even be present.

In a negotiation, of course, all sides may be concerned about the views of people not present. The colonel negotiating an agreement about environmental management on a military base probably has a general to whom she reports, who must approve the terms she negotiates—to say nothing of her lawyers and budget officers. But the indigenous group's negotiator—almost certainly coming from, having grown up in, a higher-context communication environment—may have a whole web of people and groups with whose views he must be concerned. He'll have a tribal or village council, and that's probably who he'll refer to when he says about a possible agreement: "I'll have to check." But behind, under, around, and over that council there may be all kinds of others: elders, traditional religious authorities, special societies, kin groups, matriarchs, and even spirit-entities.

The solutions to a conflict that a high-context negotiator may bring forward, or find attractive when proposed by others, may seem strange to a low-context negotiator. This is because they may not be aimed so much at resolving the issue as the low-context negotiator perceives it (for example, "how do we keep the mine from polluting the aquifer?") as they are at maintaining, honoring, strengthening, or otherwise affecting relationships. The Kawako tribal council may really *want* the Deepdark Mine to go in, for the royalty revenue it will bring to the Tribe, but they don't want it at the expense of the Tribe's relationships with the spirit world—or for the council's more acculturated members, not at the expense of the tribal council's relationship with socially powerful traditional elders. The elders, who are almost certainly not at the negotiating table but who may be in the back of the room, incognito, or have representatives there, or be consulted every evening by the negotiators, may come up with a solution that makes sense only in *their* world. You—the low-context negotiator—may find the solution very hard to accept as solving anything, but you need to be prepared to take it seriously. It may take you a long way toward agreement.

For example, when a natural gas pipeline was routed through Schultz Pass in the San Francisco Peaks—a spiritually important landscape in the eyes of the Navajo, Hopi, and other tribes and pueblos in the area—Navajo spiritual authorities advised the pipeline company and agencies involved that the impacts of construction could be addressed, at least in part, by performing a Blessingway ceremony. This was done (not necessarily a simple matter), and the project proceeded (Winter 1993, King 2003:197).

So in the case of the DeepDark Mine, there may be some cultural/spiritual activity that the company could support—a ceremony, prayers, whatever—that would resolve things from the standpoint of the Kawako elders. Let us stress that it would be utterly inappropriate—condescending and patronizing—if the negotiator for the mining company or overseeing federal agency suggested such a thing, but if the Kawako negotiators bring it up, everyone should listen carefully and give it respectful attention.

Or the solution brought forward may not be as outlandish-seeming (and inexpensive) as engaging in a ritual, but it may have nothing very obvious to do with the case or issues under discussion. Perhaps the proposal will be for the mining company to support the Tribe's traditional language program, or its environmental restoration work, or to acquire some land for the Tribe to add to its reservation. Where such a proposition is put forward, the low-context negotiator may have his own external contexts with which to deal, making sure that his lawyers or organizational superiors or oversight committee or stockholders don't see it as extortionate or illegal, but it should never be rejected out of hand. See what you can do with it.

A high-context negotiator may also insist that an agreement include what seem to a low-context person to be pointless findings, assertions, or references. For instance, an indigenous group may seek a formal acknowledgement of its sovereignty, an apology for past wrongs, or reference to a treaty, policy statement, or international accord. This language may do absolutely nothing to resolve the "real-world" problem of, say, not polluting the aquifer, but including it may be what makes agreement possible. This too is something that the agency or company negotiator is probably going to have to review with legal counsel and higher policy levels; such language can echo through the years and have unintended consequences. But again, don't brush it off as irrelevant.

Learn from the Literature

It may seem that we're lazy, but we're not going to try to outline the many, many guidelines laid out in the expansive literature on negotiation (see "Further Reading" at the end of this chapter). If you're going to be negotiating agreements, our book should not be the only one you read. Take a look at some books, articles, and websites focusing on negotiation and conflict resolution; think about how what they recommend applies to your situation. Of course, if there's a literature—including a gray literature, or oral history—about the specific groups with whom you're talking, or the specific issues you're addressing, you need to get familiar with that, too. Read the writings of, and if possible talk with, other people who have negotiated with the same or similar parties, or dealt with the same or similar issues. Try to learn from their successes and mistakes.

Don't Copy Old Models

The fact that somebody else put together an agreement that got signed five or ten (or one or two) years ago by the parties with whom you're consulting doesn't mean that it's wise for you to copy that agreement. It may be relevant to your case or it may not, and it may have worked out well or it may have been a flop. Or some parts of it may have worked while others have not, or maybe it's worked well for some parties but not for others. Or maybe it got executed and then forgotten, so it looks successful only because nobody's noticed how it's failed. Certainly you ought to look at previous agreements among your parties, or in your area, or referencing projects like yours, but look at them *critically*. Make sure you understand them, find out whether and how they've worked out, and find out how the consulting parties feel about them. Don't copy them just because they're there.

Free, Prior, and Informed Consent

Particularly if indigenous groups are among your consulting parties, you may find yourself grappling with the notion of "free, prior, and informed consent"—sometimes expressed in acronym form as FPIC. The term and acronym come from the human rights environment. They represent the principle that those in power—like governments and industries—should seek people's consent, freely given based on full information, before taking actions that affect them. Don't flood the village, log the forest, mine the mountain without getting the fully informed consent of those who live there, work there, worship there, have ancestors buried there.

In 2007, the United Nations General Assembly issued the U.N. *Declaration on the Rights of Indigenous Peoples*—which unfortunately also often goes by its acronym, UNDRIP. Several sections of the Declaration refer to FPIC, for instance:

Article 19

States shall consult and cooperate in good faith with the indigenous peoples concerned through their own representative institutions in order to obtain their *free, prior and informed consent*
before adopting and implementing legislative or administrative
measures that may affect them [emphasis added].

The words seem pretty straightforward. "Free" as in "freely given, without a gun to one's head." "Prior" as in before the fact, not after the decision's
made. "Informed" as in having all the facts, no wool pulled over the eyes.
"Consent" seems clear enough, too; it means permission. Yes or no; you *can*
do this thing or you *can't*.

The problem, of course, is that under the laws of the nations that have
approved the UNDRIP, indigenous people often don't have the legal right
to give or withhold their consent to a government or government-regulated
action. Or rather, their consent, whether given or withheld, may not have
any legal weight. Under U.S. law, for instance, federal agencies have to *consult* with Indian tribes about things they plan to do, assist, or permit that
may affect tribal concerns, but they seldom need the tribes' *consent*.

The United States, together with Australia, Canada, and New Zealand,
opposed adoption of the UNDRIP, and ignored it through the remainder
of the George W. Bush administration. Under Barack Obama, the U.S. en-
dorsed it (after similar actions by its fellow 2007 holdouts), but the State Department issued an ingenious interpretation holding that "consent" doesn't
mean giving permission. FPIC, says the State Department, means "a process of meaningful consultation with tribal leaders, but not necessarily the
agreement of those leaders".[3]

However offensive this interpretation may be to indigenous people
and fans of good English, it is certainly a fact that the UNDRIP exhorts
governments to seek FPIC, but it doesn't change anybody's laws. Understandably, though, a lot of indigenous people think that it does, or should,
have legal weight, and they may approach a negotiation with the notion that
they have approval authority when in legal fact they do not. This can create
some sticky situations. Even before UNDRIP, it was common enough to
hear tribal representatives say things like, "We've told you seventeen ways

from Sunday not to build this thing. What is it about "no" that you don't understand?" If you're negotiating for the government or the sponsor, you're faced with the problem of saying, politely, that yes, we really do hear you, and we really do understand that you're telling us "no," but we simply aren't required to take "no" for an answer, so let's talk some more and see what we can come up with. This tends not to sit well with people who feel—not without reason—that they *ought* to be able to just say "no" and make it stick.

If you're negotiating on behalf of a group that thinks that it ought to have the right to give or deny consent and have it mean something, your challenge is somehow to develop the power to make that true. The UNDRIP may help, because it represents an international consensus about what governments *ought* to do. Very publicly pointing out—or not so publicly threatening to point out— that a government agency is flying in the face of an international standard like the UNDRIP can have useful effects. But never think that your group has the right to FPIC just because the UNDRIP says it does, and never slack off in your efforts to build negotiating power just because the UNDRIP is on your side. By itself the UNDRIP is just a piece of paper; you have heavy lifting to do to make it mean anything.

Documenting Agreement

At some point in the course of negotiations, it should become apparent either that you are going to reach agreement or that you're not. Assuming the former, it's at this point that you should start talking about how the agreement should look on paper—that is, how to document or memorialize it. *Now* is the time (and not before—unless as noted above there's a strategic reason to) to begin putting together a draft.

The Art of Drafting an Agreement Document

Drafting an agreement document is something of an art. The structure and language of the document depend in substantial part on the legal authority under which agreement has been reached, and on customary practice. For example, there is very little to be found in the NHPA Section 106 regulations specifying the content or structure of a Memorandum of Agreement (MOA) on how adverse effects to historic places will be resolved, but over almost half a century of Section 106 practice, a standard format has evolved that customarily contains some fairly standard provisions. This format and these provisions for the most part are not required by law or regulation; they are simply customary. But they've become customary for a reason— they've usually been found to work, to be understandable, to be desirable. So they deserve respect and attention, though they're not written in stone, and if there are reasons not to use them, or to modify them, or to use something different, you ought to do so. Just expect that people who are used to following the customary format and including the customary provisions will probably bridle at doing anything else.

If you're doing an NHPA Section 106 agreement, you can find drafting guidance on the website of the National Preservation Institute, www.npi. org, under "Tools for Cultural Resource Managers." Most of the same guidance is in King's 2004 book, *Federal Planning and Historic Places: the Section 106 Process* (King 2004). Some of this guidance may be helpful if you're working on some other kind of agreement, but more specific direction may be found with the agencies and organizations that oversee or regularly produce agreements of the kind you're doing.

But again, be careful about using standard language, or turning to earlier agreements as models. Both can be helpful, but both can lead you astray, limit your creativity, and channel you toward proposing or agreeing to provisions that aren't quite right for your circumstances. Look at them, certainly; pay attention to them, consider them, but don't let them rule you or limit your thinking.

Leaving it to the Lawyers

If you're not a lawyer, and maybe even if you are, you'll probably need or want to have a lawyer look at your agreement, review it for what's called "legal sufficiency." Does it hang together as a legal document? Will it stand up in court? Will it be enforceable? And of course, does it propose violating any laws?

Be careful, though, about surrendering too much of your authoring authority (assuming you have any) to the lawyers. You're probably the one who really knows the case, who's been involved in the consultation from the beginning. Lawyers, however little they like to acknowledge it, are not omniscient, and they *are* servants to the managers, policy-makers, elected officials, and organizations that employ them. It's the job of those people and groups—and your job as the negotiator—to decide what can be agreed to; it's the lawyer's job to help make sure it does the legal job it's intended to do.

Write it for a Martian

Legalistic as it must be, the document's language shouldn't be incomprehensible. The agreement ought to be understandable by the people who have negotiated it and, very importantly, by those who will have to implement it. U.S. Supreme Court Justice Stephen Breyer has wisely said that when he reads a statute he first approaches it "as an English-speaking Martian would".[4] The same rule should apply to agreement documents. Ask yourself as you're writing: "Would a Martian understand this?"

Martians probably don't understand specialist jargon, so either don't use it or at least explain what your special terms mean. Martians are notorious for being confused by acronyms, so at least give them a key. Martians (having just landed) don't have access to insider information on the background of your agreement and what's led up to it. Try to make sure the background is explained somewhere—either in the agreement document itself or in referenced supporting documents. But Martians are also easily bored and distracted, so we advise against lengthy introductions or prologues to agreements. Agreements are contracts binding their parties; they should be clear, succinct, and to the point. Refer to other documents— environmental impact assessments, survey reports, whatever—for details. Agreement documents also seldom need appended dictionaries or glossaries. If terms are already defined in law or regulation, or in literature, simply cite them as such; if they're not, and they're esoteric or otherwise subject to misinterpretation, then a short definition will suffice. There's no need to go on and on.

Remember that you're not writing the agreement just for yourself and the individuals with whom you've negotiated it. Even if you're currently charged with implementing the agreement, you may get crushed tomorrow by an errant Martian spacecraft, in which case somebody else would have to take over and interpret what you've written. And the thing may be interpreted by courts of law, maybe long, long after it's written, by people from still other planets.

Be Wary of Can-Kicking

One of the easiest things in the world to agree upon is to put something off, and consulting parties often take this easy way out in an agreement. For example, the agreement will be made to provide for the subsequent development of a plan to do something—further explore some mitigation option, perhaps, or better define a sensitive resource. Sometimes this is a responsible, necessary thing to do, but often it amounts simply to kicking the can down the road; it accomplishes nothing except to delay resolution of whatever issues are the subjects of consultation. Or it obviates the whole consultation by breaking the connection between conflict and cause. "We'll do a plan to perform a study of how to resolve this problem—but in the meantime we can approve the project, which is what is causing the problem in the first place." This kind of can-kicking is irresponsible at best. At worst, it's a way to pull the wool over the consulting parties' eyes and blast on with the project. It can be very tempting, but if you're trying to consult in good faith, you should resist the temptation. If you're a party being consulted, you need to scrutinize whatever is put before you like a hawk seeking field mice, and if you see something that looks like a can-kick, swoop on it without mercy. Ask why the proposed study or finding or review is really needed, and don't accept vague answers. Most importantly, if the put-off really is necessary, make sure that it's going to be completed, and its results factored into decision-making *before* the critical decisions are made.

Where it *is* necessary to put something off pending some kind of further study or planning, the consulting parties—especially those whose concerns may or may not be addressed as a result of whatever is put off—should be careful to stipulate how the study or planning will be done, when it will be done, by whom it will be done, and how it will relate to decision making. Perhaps it really is impossible to be sure that a seemingly feasible means of drilling through the PaleAle Aquifer without polluting it will actually work, and some kind of adaptive management[5] program may be proposed. The Kawako and NIMBI, if they're inclined to accept this proposal or unable to resist it, ought at least to make sure—if they can—that assessment of the technique's success is a matter of mutual fact-finding in which they participate. They ought also to make sure—if they can—that if the technique does *not* work, its employment will be halted and the parties will come back to the table to consider alternatives, including terminating the project.

Multiple Authors

Sometimes different consulting parties will draft different sections of the agreement document, and then somebody will cobble it all together. There's nothing wrong with this, and it may make a lot of sense if the agreement deals with several different issues or topics, on which different parties have expertise. However, it can create a pretty lumpy document, and introduce opportunities for inconsistent and even contradictory language. If you use multiple authors, be sure that somebody is responsible for overall editorial control, so you don't wind up, for instance, referring to the same place, process, or thing by several different names.

Finalizing

Your document may go through several drafts, circulated among the parties for their consideration and editing. This can be very tedious, and try everyone's patience, but there's no way we know of to avoid it. Electronic file sharing helps speed things up, of course, but it also introduces lots of opportunities for error. Collaborative editing software can minimize such opportunities, but everyone has to have access to it, and we have yet to see that be the case. Right now, we muddle through as best we can, and finalizing an agreement document tends to be a pretty murky process.

Once you have a draft—depending on how contentious the issues are— it often makes sense to have a face-to-face, or at least a telephonic or cyber-space meeting to go through it point by point to make sure everyone shares an understanding of it, and to resolve any remaining ambiguities.

Make Sure the Right People Sign

Once you finally do have a document that the parties are ready to sign, make sure it's signed by the right people—that is, by the people who actually have the authority to do so on behalf of their organizations. This is especially important with respect to whoever is going to implement the agreement. If the agreement says that the DeepDark Mining Company is going to pay six million ducats to buy the SweetRunning Spring and turn it over to the Kawako Tribe, you need to make sure that whoever signs for DeepDark can really commit the company to spend the money. Or that whoever signs for the government agency whose permission DeepDark needs to put in the mine has the authority to insist that the company cough up the ducats. That may seem pretty obvious, but you might be surprised at how often U.S. government agencies decide that their "cultural resource" experts (who usually have no authority to commit the agencies to anything) ought to sign NHPA Section 106 agreements, because after all, they're the experts. When it comes to signing an agreement document, expertise is irrelevant; what matters is, can the signer deliver on his or her signature?

Delivering

Delivering, of course, is what seeking agreement is all about. There's not much point in even trying to reach agreement if the agreement that's reached won't be implemented. It might surprise you—or then again, it might not—how often people who negotiate to resolve cultural and environmental conflicts figure the agreement documents they write will implement themselves, and how often those documents actually just get filed and forgotten.

You can increase the likelihood that your agreement will actually be implemented by including provisions for doing so in the document you draft. Specify deadlines, and require progress reports to the consulting parties, and perhaps annual or monthly reviews. Make sure the agreement document has a "drop dead" or "sunset" clause, under which it becomes null and void, and the parties have to come back to the table, if it's not implemented by X date.

Be absolutely sure that the document clearly assigns responsibilities. Try to avoid using passive voice; don't say, "the Great Green Tree will be inspected by a licensed arborist," but say, "the Timber Management Service will ensure that the Great Green Tree is inspected by a licensed arborist by April 15, 2025."

Be clear about what the responsibility is. In the above example, what is the arborist supposed to do? Stipulate this by saying something like: "—to determine the Great Green Tree's health and probable lifespan, and will file a report with all the consulting parties within thirty (30) days after the inspection is completed."

Speaking of reports—if the agreement will be implemented over a period of months or years, or if it involves several disparate activities, perhaps carried out by different parties, you'll probably need to stipulate how reports will be prepared, circulated, and reviewed. Maybe they'll be annual reports, or quar-

terly, or monthly, or maybe they'll be on particular actions—say, the completion of a landscaping program or plans for the rehabilitation of a building. You
may also need to provide for meetings of parties to the agreement, or others, to
discuss the report and decide whether changes need to be made.

From which it follows that you're likely to need some mechanism for resolving disagreements—when the Kawako say the landscaping plan for the
spring is fine but NIMBI says it's not, or when somebody else (who may not
have been a party to the agreement) looks at the landscaping and thinks its
dreadful. Make sure to provide ways to resolve disputes like these that may
arise over interpretation or implementation of the agreement.

Don't assume that some unspecified policing authority will make sure
the agreement is implemented properly. In the United States, consulting parties on NHPA Section 106 agreements sometimes act as though they think
the State Historic Preservation Officer (SHPO) has an enforcement budget
and officers walking the beat—which no SHPO in fact has. Unless in your
case there really *is* a legally constituted, adequately funded enforcement body,
try to put systems in place to make sure what's been agreed to actually happens. Do you need to contract with someone, like an arborist in the example
above? Get together with your contracting people and figure out how to do
it. Are you committed to annual reports? Make sure preparing the report
each year is in your calendar, that you know what's involved in producing
it, and that you gather the resources and people to do it in a timely manner.

Don't forget that you're not immortal. Make sure that if you're run over
by a Martian spacecraft next month or next year, someone else will know
that they have to take over implementing the agreement, and that they'll
have the tools necessary to do so.

Once the agreement is signed (if it's signed), make sure it's put someplace
where it can be found and referred to, and where it won't be lost or forgotten.
Here again, don't assume that there's some wonderful archive somewhere
that automatically files agreements and makes them available on demand.
There almost certainly isn't, so you'll probably have to improvise. Talk about
it as you bring the consultation to a close. How *will* we make sure that our
successors, or the public, or the courts, know how to find this agreement and
its supporting data, so they can refer to it when needed? If nothing else, make
sure that all parties to the agreement get a fully executed copy of it, in a form
that they can easily file.

If you're *not* the one responsible for implementing the agreement—if you're another consulting party, or just a consultant to one of the parties—you obviously can't make all these things happen, but you ought to remind others of their responsibilities and do what you can to make sure they carry them out. One of the frustrations that we've both faced as consultants, though, is that our contracts end and we really don't have much choice but to walk away and hope that whatever we've negotiated is carried out. Since the carrying-out may take years and years, it's up to those who remain on the scene to make sure that what they provide for really happens. Implementation ought to be the job of whoever's responsible for the project that's been the focus of the consultation, but the rest of the consulting parties shouldn't be too trusting about this. If you can, set up your own systems for monitoring what the project sponsor does, and don't let him forget that you're looking over his shoulder.

What If There's No Agreement?

Any time there's the possibility of reaching agreement, there's naturally the possibility of not agreeing. Exactly what happens when consulting parties fail to agree depends on the legal context in which the disagreement happens—the laws and regulations that apply.

At one end of the spectrum are laws like the U.S. Endangered Species Act (ESA)—where, as you'll recall, consultation is only between the responsible agency and either the Fish and Wildlife Service or the National Marine Fisheries Service. Under the ESA the cards are all pretty much in the hands of the two services. In cases where agreement isn't reached on ways to prevent undue endangerment, consultation winds up with one of them issuing a Biological Opinion containing "recommendations" that the responsible agency pretty much has to follow. Various state level endangered species acts are similarly structured. Where a government agency has the authority to issue a permit of any kind, the situation is much the same; there may be consultation along the way, but in the end the agency either issues the permit or doesn't, subject to whatever conditions it chooses to impose.

At the other end of the spectrum, where consultations (if there are any) under a law like the National Environmental Policy Act (NEPA) don't lead to agreement, the responsible agency can simply consider the results of consultation to the extent it thinks right, and then make its decision about whether and how to go forward with the project. In the final analysis, the agency can blow off the disagreement, and doesn't really even have to consult.

Somewhere in the middle lies consultation under something like the NHPA Section 106 regulations. Under Section 106 there are strong incen-tives to reach agreement, but if agreement isn't reached, then the responsible federal agency is required to seek the comments of the ACHP. The ACHP's comments go to the head of the responsible federal agency—usually a cabinet secretary or equivalent—who must give the comments her personal consideration and make a decision. The agency head doesn't have to do what the ACHP says she should do—the ACHP is advisory, after all. But the ACHP is itself made up mostly of federal agency heads and presidential appointees, and it gets some measure of respect. So the tendency is to try at least to go part-way toward what the ACHP recommends. And since no federal agency employee wants a high-level council telling his boss that he's done wrong,[6] there's a good deal of pressure to make a deal before the matter reaches the agency head.

Whatever the results of consultation, it's wise to document them so there's an administrative record for future reference. Some government agencies have detailed procedures for creating and filing such documentation, while others do not. If you have no procedures to follow, let a variant on the Golden Rule be your guide: if you were consulting someone's documentation fifty or a hundred years into the future, how would you like it to be organized and compiled?

FURTHER READING ON NEGOTIATION

Cohen, Raymond

1997 *Negotiating Across Cultures: International Communication in an Interdependent World.* Washington D.C., Institute of Peace Press.

> Although Cohen's examples are drawn from the world of international diplomacy, the principles he articulates are relevant to any cross-cultural negotiation; he usefully corrects and adjusts some of the narrowly Euroamerican assumptions on which Fisher et al. based *Getting to Yes* (discussed later in this list).

Dorochoff, Nicholas

2007   *Negotiation Basics for Cultural Resource Managers.* Walnut Creek, CA, Left Coast Press, Inc.

A short, plain-language guide to negotiation under federal, state, and local historic preservation and cultural resource management laws in the United States.

Fisher, Roger, William Ury and Bruce Patton

2011   *Getting to Yes: Negotiating Agreement Without Giving In*, Revised Edition. New York, Penguin Press.

The granddaddy of negotiation books; still a good read with much to teach. Outlines many of the fundamental concepts and methods of negotiative consultation, simply and clearly. Cohen (1997) cautions that it is written from the viewpoint of a low-context negotiator, and the techniques it recommends don't necessarily work very well across cultural boundaries.

Innes, Judith E. and David E. Booher

2010   *Planning with Complexity: An Introduction to Collaborative Rationality for Public Policy.* New York, Routledge.

A very important, thought-stimulating book outlining the theory and practice of collaborative decision-making. Most relevant to situations in which the participants are somehow interdependent and faced with a set of problems that they understand to be "wicked"—i.e., complicated by the numbers of interests involved, contradictory or incomplete data, their interconnections with other problems, and/or the heavy economic burdens involved—but with much food for thought even for those involved in more routine kinds of consultation.

Shell, G. Richard

2006   *Bargaining for Advantage: Negotiation Strategies for Reasonable People,* 2nd Edition. New York, Penguin.

Deals with both collaborative or joint gain seeking negotiation—the preferred approach in *Getting to Yes* and *Planning with*

Complexity—and the more aggressive adversarial or advantage-seeking approach with which most of us, sadly, are more familiar.

Ury, William

1993   *Getting Past No: Negotiating in Difficult Situations.* New York, Bantam.

Often used as a companion to *Getting to Yes*, *Getting Past No* focuses on how to deal with cases in which agreement appears to be unattainable.

CHAPTER 7

Reasoning Together—or Not

How to End It?

Nissley and King have argued a bit about this concluding chapter. King's impulse was to conclude with a tongue-in-cheek outline of ways a project sponsor or agency official can *avoid* consultation, or at least keep it from influencing decision-making. Nissley called for a more upbeat conclusion, providing real-world examples of successful consultations. King's response was "right, so show me some." While positive examples do exist, they are often complicated, hard to explain, and somewhat dependent on special circumstances. They also tend to have produced equivocal results.

It should be no surprise that even the most "successful" consultations are not successes in everybody's eyes. They almost always produce compromises—which may be in the broad public interest but seldom make everyone (or anyone) happy. And the resolutions they produce are always specific to the circumstances of the particular case, which notably include the individuals involved. It is not uncommon for participants in a generally satisfactory consultation to say, "we made no progress at all until X retired/resigned/was fired/died." It's not very helpful to hold up as a model of consultation one in which the parties had to wait for a resolution until one of their number kicked off or got canned.

After a good deal of pondering and bickering, it occurred to us that we actually did know of one at least fairly good, reasonably successful consultation—indeed, we had both participated in it. Although by no means perfect, it does provide a basis for tying together what we've discussed in the previous chapters and outlining some basic principles of effective consultation.

Meanwhile, current world events have given us a counter-example showing what can happen when a powerful agent of change elects *not* to

Claudia Nissley and Thomas F. King, "Reasonong Together—Or Not" in *Consultation and Cultural Heritage: Let Us Reason Together*, pp. 120-134. © 2014 Left Coast Press, Inc. All rights reserved.

consult. Whatever this example's eventual result, it provides a cautionary tale that we think is worth the reader's contemplation.

A Fairly Good Consultation:
Non-Native Fish Management in the Grand Canyon

In the 1950s and 60s, the U.S. Bureau of Reclamation built Glen Canyon Dam across the Colorado River upstream of the Grand Canyon. The resulting reservoir was stocked with rainbow and brown trout for the enjoyment of anglers. Over the years trout have escaped and established themselves downriver, where they are thought to pose a threat to the native, endangered humpback chub. So in 2009, at the direction of the U.S. Fish and Wildlife Service under the U.S. Endangered Species Act, the Bureau proposed a program of "mechanical removal" under which some 20,000 trout per year would be stunned with electric shocks, sucked out of the water and ground up for fertilizer. The removal was to take place at the confluence of the Little Colorado and Colorado Rivers, in the Grand Canyon.

In the beliefs of the Hualapai, Hopi, Navajo, Southern Paiute and Zuni tribes, the Grand Canyon is a very powerful cultural landscape. Some believe that their ancestors emerged into this world from another through the Canyon at the beginning of time. Some associate the Canyon, or specific places in it, with potent spirits and spirit-forces. Some collect necessary plants, animals, and minerals in the Canyon, including those associated with healing and the acquisition of esoteric knowledge. All recount important traditions associated with the Canyon, and use such stories to teach life-lessons to their youth. The confluence of the Colorado and Little Colorado figures centrally in many of the tribal traditions. For all these reasons, the Grand Canyon in its entirety is understood by the Bureau, the National Park Service, and other involved federal agencies to be eligible for the National Register of Historic Places (NRHP). The agencies have been known to lose this understanding from time to time, but the tribes remind them.

When the Bureau informed the tribes of the fish-removal plan, the Zuni were particularly upset. Zuni believe that they have family relationships with all aquatic life, so grinding up the fish would be like killing Zuni children. The fact that the trout were not native to the Canyon was irrelevant, they were living creatures and they would be wantonly killed. Examining the scientific data upon which the removal plan was based, Zuni experts also found it lacking in rigor, characterizing the premise that the trout were wiping out the chub as little more than a "hunch." The tribal council enacted a resolution against the removal project, emphasizing the tribe's spiritual relationships with the fish and pointing out the Canyon's eligibility for the NRHP. The other tribes, for somewhat varying reasons and with varying levels of intensity, supported the Zuni.

Based on its understanding that the Canyon was eligible for the NRHP and that its fish contributed to its eligibility, the Bureau initiated consultation with the tribes, State Historic Preservation Officer (SHPO) and others under Section 106 of the U.S. National Historic Preservation Act (NHPA). And it did, we think, a pretty creditable job (which admittedly included hiring us to help). Here, in simplified form, is how it worked, with reference to the components of consultation set forth in the NHPA Section 106 definition and discussed in the preceding chapters.

Seeking Views

The Bureau had already established communication with the tribes, SHPO, and other interested parties, and had a good understanding of its responsibility to engage in government-to-government consultation. So as it undertook environmental impact assessment under the National Environmental Policy Act (NEPA) it began consultation. It did so by sending information on its proposal to all concerned, having a number of meetings, and suggesting discussions aimed at developing agreement. The very negative reactions of the Zuni and other tribes led the Bureau to decide that it needed assistance, so it engaged the services of Nissley and King, with and through Mary Orton, a professional facilitator/mediator.

Nissley attended a meeting between the Bureau and the Zuni Tribal Council that highlighted the seriousness of the tribes' concern, and we made email and telephone contact with the Zuni and other consulting parties to gain first impressions of their points of view. The Bureau had also developed a good deal of background documentation during NEPA review to date, much of which laid out consulting parties' concerns or impressions of those concerns. In conference calls and correspondence with Bureau personnel we tried to organize all this into a coherent roadmap for consultation.

Discussing Views

The Bureau invited all the consulting parties to a multi-day meeting[1] to discuss their concerns and see what progress could be made toward resolving their disagreements. The meeting was facilitated by Orton, with Nissley and King providing support. Virtually all the parties—tribes, SHPO, federal and state agencies—took part, though some (for instance, sport fishermen interested in the trout population) elected not to.

The meeting was free-wheeling, with everyone able to state their views and get them addressed. Our initial role was to help each party understand what the others were saying, and to try to get each to clarify its answers to questions and challenges.

It became clear that the tribes—particularly the Zuni—simply did not accept the ostensibly scientific finding that the trout were overwhelming the chub, and objected absolutely to what some called the Bureau's "fish whacking" proposal. The Fish and Wildlife Service made it equally clear that it intended to stand by its opinion that the trout had to be reduced—whatever the questions about its methods. The Bureau was more or less caught in the middle, trying to respect the tribes' values and concerns, but having to meet its responsibilities under the Endangered Species Act as interpreted by the Fish and Wildlife Service. The SHPO, National Park Service, and others offered suggestions about ways to resolve the dispute, which were discussed at length.

Considering Views

The Bureau's consideration of tribal and other views began well before the meeting, and continued during and after it. During the meeting the Bureau conducted itself as just another consulting party, participating on an equal basis with all the others. As the meeting progressed, the shape of a possible agreement began to emerge, and the Bureau's representatives let us know that it was one with which they could live. Nissley's and King's roles shifted subtly from trying to help the parties clarify their own interests and understand those of others, to helping try out options for agreement.

Seeking Agreement

Partway through the meeting, with the concurrence of the parties, we roughed out the form of an NHPA Section 106 Memorandum of Agreement (MOA). The conferees then moved into discussing its terms. A number of changes were made to the draft, and at last a general, tentative agreement was reached that an MOA roughly coincident with its terms would, perhaps, be acceptable to all concerned.

Agreement in the field turned out to be one thing, however, and agreement within the Department of the Interior (of which the Bureau, the Fish and Wildlife Service, and the National Park Service are parts) quite another. When the MOA was cleaned up and sent to Washington D.C. for review, some of the Department's lawyers objected to the notion that Fish and Wildlife Service opinions should be open to any kind of consultation. Some of the Bureau's "cultural resource" staff expressed alarm at the idea of the whole Grand Canyon as a landscape eligible for the NRHP, and of fish as contributing to its cultural significance. Things bogged down, but eventually a somewhat watered-down MOA went back to the other consulting parties for review. The tribes gave way on some points but held firm on others, and at last an MOA was executed (see Appendix 3).

The MOA explicitly recognized the cultural significance of the Canyon, the Colorado River, and the fish, and expressed agreement among the federal agencies and SHPO that the Canyon was eligible for the NRHP. Its key provision was that the Bureau would remove and relocate trout alive (if it removed them at all), and that all such removals would be carried out in consultation with the tribes, who could elect to participate in or monitor the removal activities. If live removal turned out not to stabilize the chub population, then the Bureau would consult again about "acceptable mitigation," which presumably might allow for killing the trout, but only after further consultation.

In our opinion the final MOA is a good deal vaguer than it ought to be on a number of points, but this was probably inevitable. The draft that went to Washington included provisions for studies to validate or not validate the science on which the Fish and Wildlife Service's opinions were based, as a prerequisite to any consideration of mechanical removal. This must have been threatening to the Service, so it was deleted in favor of not mentioning mechanical removal at all. The draft MOA also provided for an explicit effort to integrate the tribes' traditional ecological knowledge into fish habitat management; this provision was probably deleted as irrelevant, in favor of a general provision for elective tribal participation in fish removal. But every agreement of this kind is a compromise, and this one seems essentially to have—thus far—accomplished its purpose. Fish management in the Grand Canyon is going on with tribal participation, the trout are not being sucked out of the river and chopped up, and the chub are apparently none the worse for it all.

What Makes This a Good Consultation?

No consultation is perfect, but the Fish Management MOA consultation was, we think, a pretty good one, for at least the following reasons.

Things Not Done

The Bureau—at least until Washington got involved—refrained from doing some truly stupid things that many another agency has done under similar circumstances.

For one thing, it did not insist that the Grand Canyon was just too big, or two vaguely defined, or too natural to be eligible for the NRHP, or that fish couldn't be considered as contributing to its cultural significance because they're—well, fish. This would have derailed the consultation before it ever got started, and would have accomplished nothing other than to comfort some narrow minds on the Bureau's staff.

For another, it didn't argue that the Zuni concern about non-native fish killing was beyond consideration because it wasn't "scientific," or because the trout weren't native. This would have been a biased, ethnocentric position, but it is not unlike the one taken by the U.S. Ninth Circuit Court of Appeals in finding that whatever the tribes of the area say, their religious practices are not burdened by spraying the sacred San Francisco Peaks with artificial snow derived from urine (in *Navajo Nation v. U.S. Forest Service*; see King 2010 for discussion). This too would have brought consultation to a screeching halt.

Things Done

The things the Bureau did right, we'd say, included at least the following:

1. Taking the time necessary to figure out what everybody thought, and bringing everybody together to reason about the matter;

2. Involving relatively high-level policy makers as well as the folks on the ground who knew the case and had the necessary decision-making contacts (though the lawyers and Washington staff should have been brought in, and gotten under control, at the outset—if this was possible);

3. Treating the tribes and other parties with respect, and honoring their cultural interests and differences;

4. Getting the help needed—in this case Orton, Nissley, and King, but there were and are plenty of other options—to help keep the consultation moving;

5. Devoting the resources (money, time, effort) to make it all happen; and

6. Generally being flexible, open to ideas and arguments, and sensitive to the varying cultural concerns and capacities of the parties.

Some Principles

Beyond the specific things the Bureau of Reclamation did and refrained from doing, we think the Grand Canyon case elucidates some larger principles that ought to guide us when we undertake consultation.

PRINCIPLE 1 **None of us is God.** We're not omniscient, not omnipotent; we haven't been around since the beginning of days and we certainly can't see the future. If God can offer to reason together, then surely so can we. Consultation ought not to be just a necessary bureaucratic chore, a box to tick off on a checklist. It ought to be a reasoning together, a cooperative effort to identify and resolve issues. In the world of environmental impact assessment and cultural resource management, it ought to be about figuring out and resolving the impacts a project may have on the natural and cultural environment, and particularly on what matters about that environment to people.

Our employers and clients aren't God, either, however much they may want to be treated as though they were. Those who work for or advise project sponsors and oversight agencies do them no favors by portraying consultation to them as a mere procedural requirement. Treating it as such may work a good deal of the time, but every now and then it won't, and when it doesn't, the results can be very, very costly. Our clients and our bosses are better advised to approach consultation honestly, creatively, and with attention to the Golden Rule, so that's how we ought to advise them.

PRINCIPLE 2 **A Made-Up Mind Impedes (or Dooms) Consultation.** In the Grand Canyon case, the biggest impediments to successful consultation were made-up minds. The Fish and Wildlife Service was convinced that the trout were eating—or at least outcompeting with—the chub, and that the appropriate scientific—and therefore good and proper—way to deal with them was by sucking and grinding them up. The Bureau's and Department's lawyers in Washington were convinced that the Service's determinations could not, should not, must not be subjected to "non-scientific" scrutiny. Archaeologists in the Bureau were scandalized at the idea of treating the whole Grand Canyon, with its fish, as a historic property based on its cultural significance to tribes. These made-up minds came close to derailing the consultation.

Of course, the minds of the Zuni tribal government and elders were pretty much made up, too; it was certain to them, based on centuries-old traditional belief (their science), that killing the fish was a really bad idea. But they demonstrated a good deal of flexibility in their willingness even to consider the idea of mechanical removal as long as it wasn't done around the junction of the Colorado and Little Colorado Rivers. And—here's a subprinciple—it's not unreasonable to begin consultation with a pretty limited range of acceptable options if (a) you're consulting from a position of relative weakness and need to make a vivid point, and/or if (b) the options being discussed will have major impacts on your deeply-felt cultural values. It's fair to say that in the Colorado River case, it was the firmness of the Zuni and other tribes about the impacts of mechanical removal that eventually overcame (to some extent) the inflexibility of the government's lawyers, scientists, and historic preservation experts.

PRINCIPLE 3 **All Solutions Deserve a Fair Shot.** For consultation to be meaningful, each party must have a fighting chance to prevail. Inevitably, some will have more power than others, which can't help but give them a better chance than those with less power, but if those in charge of the consultation want it to be fair (a big "if," of course), there must be at least some possibility that a solution or solutions proposed by the less powerful parties will in the end be adopted.

In the Grand Canyon case, the federal agencies had the great bulk of the power, and in the end could impose their solutions, but the tribes had something of an equalizer in their status as sovereign nations to which the U.S. government has a "trust" or fiduciary responsibility—the federal government is responsible for protecting their interests, so it can't too blithely squash them.

However, the trust responsibility has been most often and easily attended to when the interests involved were more or less economic or at least quantifiable—such as rights to water or fish, or the management of a mineral estate. If the Zuni or other tribes had to try to stop mechanical fish removal in court based on the government's trust responsibility, it's not clear how they would fare. But none of the parties wanted to go to court. So, as previously discussed, the Bureau put the necessary resources into holding a pretty thorough and honest consultation, and gave respectful weight to the tribes' point of view. While the Zuni's preferred option of backing completely away from mechanical removal pending more and better science did not prevail, it was the top contender until Washington got involved. The tribe's second-best option, live removal until and unless it proves ineffective, *did* prevail.

Recreational fishermen and the commercial firms that serve them were notable by their absence from the consultation, though their interests—presumably involving trout in the river—must have been subject to effect by its outcome. Presumably they sat out the meetings because they saw no utility in taking part, and/or because they figured that any consultation carried out under historic preservation laws and regulations really had nothing to do with them. In shunning consultation, though, they left their interests in the hands of others, and their interests got very little consideration. Had they participated, they might have added weight to the case against mechanical removal, being able to advance arguments that were different from those of the tribes but at least mostly complementary to them. This highlights another principle.

PRINCIPLE 4 **Everyone Should Be At the Table.** Even if the law requires—or can be taken to require—consultation only with experts, government officials, indigenous groups, or some other limited range of parties, it's better to consult with everyone concerned. It may not be possible to have everyone literally at the same table, in the same meeting room, but everyone with interests ought somehow to be consulted, and have the opportunity to have their views prevail. From this follows another principle.

PRINCIPLE 5 **Comprehensive Beats Special-Purpose Consultation.** The U.S. legal system is a hodge-podge when it comes to consultation about things like environmental impacts; various laws, executive orders, and regulations mandate consultation with different parties under different circumstances. But we're more likely to reach a mutually agreeable conclusion if we try to consult comprehensively, holistically, instead of bit by bit, piece by piece.

Most of the consultation in which we've been involved in our careers has been done under the authority of NHPA Section 106, so technically it's been limited to the narrow question of how to characterize and resolve impacts on "historic places." If one interprets this term narrowly it can be taken to mean only old buildings and archaeological sites. Had the Bureau of Reclamation interpreted it that way in the Grand Canyon case, it would have had no way to use the Section 106 consultation process to address and resolve the issues that concerned the Zuni and other tribes. The Bureau was able to deal with these concerns by interpreting historic places to include expansive cultural landscapes like the Grand Canyon with its fish. Its consultation with the Fish and Wildlife Service under the Endangered Species Act, on the other hand, was much more narrowly constrained, and the results of that consultation—the direction to undertake mechanical removal—was what caused the problem with the tribes.

It would be better, we believe, if there were a simpler, more comprehensive law than the NHPA that required consultation with people about their cultural-environmental concerns—something like Rio Tinto's internal guidelines (Rio Tinto 2011) or the *Akwé Kon* guidelines of the Center for Biological Diversity (SCBD 2004) but without all the caveats and limitations those documents contain. But in the United States, at least, there isn't, so we, and agencies like the Bureau of Reclamation, make do with the NHPA and the even thinner, more limited consultation guidance provided by NEPA. In most other countries similar adaptations are necessary. The laws tend to focus on particular types of resource (e.g., historic places), or groups of people (e.g., Indian tribes), but good practice dictates casting a broader net. Which raises another principle, or perhaps just a bit of advice.

PRINCIPLE 6 **Comprehensive Consultation *Can* Be Made to Happen.** It's probably safe to say that the Bureau of Reclamation would not have opted to address fish removal under NHPA Section 106 if the Zuni and other tribes hadn't forced the issue. Had the fishermen gotten into the consultation and developed an understanding of what Section 106 is about, they might have made the consultation more comprehensive still, and improved the result for themselves, for the tribes, and for the fish.

Few agencies are as broad-minded as the Bureau of Reclamation was in the Grand Canyon case; most try to keep their NHPA Section 106 consultations focused narrowly on old buildings and archaeological sites, and minimize consultation under other laws altogether. As we write this the Bureau of Land Management, for instance—another sister agency of Reclamation's—continues to resist addressing the cultural value of wild horse and burro habitat under Section 106, and the Fish and Wildlife Service is backing away from a prior decision to treat Bald Eagle nesting areas as places eligible for the National Register. This means, of course, that people with cultural investments in wild horses and burros or eagles will not have access to the consultative requirements of Section 106. They won't, that is, unless they, like the Zuni in the Grand Canyon case, stand up and insist on it, and make knowledgeable use of the regulatory, legal, and political processes to force government to pay attention.

PRINCIPLE 7 **Consultation Should Have an End-Point.** Although it sometimes seems to be, consultation is not an end in itself. It should have a definite purpose, and proceed rationally toward attaining it. This is not to say that the end should be pre-determined, as so often happens in environmental impact assessment and when an agency or sponsor drafts a NHPA Section 106 Memorandum of Agreement before initiating consultation. At some point, however, if it appears that agreement can be reached, work should begin on memorializing it. If it cannot be reached, then it may be time to give up and trigger whatever mechanism the law affords for otherwise bringing discussion to a close. In the Grand Canyon case, the understood purpose of consultation from the start was to seek a Memorandum of Agreement, and that purpose was eventually achieved. Had agreement not been reached, the Bureau could have terminated consultation, obtained the comments of the Advisory Council on Historic Preservation, and then made a decision about whether and how to proceed.

PRINCIPLE 8 **Any Agreement Reached Should be Implemented.** At the time of this writing, to the best of our knowledge the terms of the Grand Canyon MOA are being implemented. If any fish removal is going on, it is live removal. Communication is continuing between the Bureau and the tribes, as well as with other consulting parties. Something may derail implementation down the road, but if so, the MOA provides for the parties to reconvene and consult further about what to do. Any consultation should result in some such written, signed agreement, and should include provision for what to do if circumstances change. Then the parties need to pay careful attention to how the terms of the agreement are carried out.

The Grand Canyon Case as Collaborative Reasoning

In many ways, the Grand Canyon case—unlike most with which we routinely deal—approximates Innes and Booher's (2010) model of collaborative reasoning. The key parties were somewhat interdependent. The tribes have no choice but to depend on the federal agencies—that control the land—to care for the Canyon, the Colorado River, its plants and animals and cultural/spiritual qualities. The agencies are more or less bound by their fiduciary responsibilities to the tribes, by their conservation mandates, and by public opinion to pay attention to the tribes' concerns and to the environment. As a result, they devoted the time, resources, and brainpower needed to conduct an open, freewheeling consultation. It's doubtful whether the tribes would like to characterize the consultation and its results as "collaboration"—a rather suspect term in Indian country—but the process did work more or less as Innes and Booher prescribe.

This raises an obvious question: why can we not make more of our consultations resemble collaborative reasoning? The most obvious answer is that the parties usually are not interdependent; sponsors and oversight agencies hold most of the cards, and in the end can deal them according to their own priorities and world-views, after giving what passes for due consideration to the views of others. It's difficult, often impossible, to level the playing field. And collaborative processes do take time, do cost money. It can be questioned whether they take *more* time, or cost *more* money, than forging ahead with projects on whose formulation stakeholders have not truly collaborated, but the costs of an ill-conceived project's delays, complications, and failures may be hidden by an agency's or company's accounting practices, and are hard to compare with the more obvious costs of hiring a facilitator, holding meetings, and conducting collaborative studies.

Improvements could be achieved, however, if the governmental bodies responsible for overseeing project review under environmental and cultural resource laws gave systematic thought to how to make such review more collaborative, learned about collaborative processes, and adjusted their review procedures accordingly. We can hope for such improvements, but are not inclined to hold our breaths.

In the Absence of Consultation: Gezi Park, Istanbul, Turkey

As we were beginning work on these last chapters, in June of 2013, the news media were rather belatedly covering a crisis in Turkey. Presumably it will be resolved, one way or another, by the time anyone reads this book, but it provides such an object lesson in the results of poor (or nonexistent) consultation that it provides a fitting counterpoint to the Grand Canyon case.

Gezi Park is a modest-sized rectangle of trees and other greenery extending north from Taksim Square, the central plaza of Istanbul's Beyoğlu district. It occupies the site of an Ottoman era artillery barracks, demolished in 1940. It's about the only substantial piece of green space in Beyoğlu, a cosmopolitan neighborhood on the northeast side of the Golden Horn. It has become a popular gathering place for local people, somewhat distinct from Taksim Square itself with its big Monument of the Republic and swarms of tourists. It must be an important part of the local cultural fabric, an urban amenity that people value.

Prime Minister Recep Tayyip Erdoğan wants to rip out the park and put in a reconstruction of the artillery barracks, which will house a shopping mall. In late May of 2013, opponents of the plan who valued the park occupied the site, protesting the development. On May 31, police firing tear gas and water cannons attacked them, and within hours there were massive protests in cities all over Turkey.

At this writing it is unclear how the matter will be resolved, but Taksim Square seems destined to join Tiananmen and Tahrir Squares as symbols of early twenty-first century revolt against perceived government oppression. The Turkish uprising spread far beyond Istanbul and the local issues of environmental protection, historic preservation, and urban planning that touched it off, but it is safe to say that it would not have happened, or at least would have happened later, elsewhere, in response to something else, if the Erdoğan government had been smarter, and a bit more humble, about trying to have its way.

On June 3, BBC News ran a televised interview with a man in the Istanbul street, an avowed supporter of the Prime Minister, who said, "I like the Prime Minister a lot, but anyone can make mistakes. He should have consulted the people."

The Prime Minister's response to reminders like this has been to point to his 51 percent electoral majorities and say that in a democracy, if people don't like what their leaders do, they vote them out of office. There's some truth in that, but it reflects a pretty primitive notion of democratic process. As we finish work on this chapter, the whole matter is in the courts. The park still stands and is used by people under the watchful eyes of plainclothes police. No one knows how the case will turn out, or what further conflicts a final decision (if there is one) may spawn, but it is certainly a fact that the Gezi Park affair has tarnished Turkey's and Erdoğan's reputations as models of governance in the contemporary Middle East.

As far as we can tell—admittedly from a considerable distance—the Prime Minister and his colleagues did little or no consultation with the local and other people who value Gezi Park. They developed the project plans and got them approved by the local government, and then fired up the bulldozers. When people objected, they were branded as "terrorists" and "outside agitators," and eventually dispersed with tear gas, water cannons, and hundreds of heavily armed and armored police. Many were imprisoned, many injured, some killed. The police took casualties too, reportedly including some suicides by officers ashamed of what they were ordered to do.

Can we imagine a different approach, with, perhaps, a happier outcome?

Suppose that the Prime Minister's representatives had brought the mall/armory proposal to the people of Beyoğlu and sat down to talk about it. They would almost certainly have learned that people are very attached to Gezi Park, and that the alternative of a commercial facility inside an ersatz historic building did not greatly attract them. The Prime Minister could have taken this fact into account in making a decision about the project—before being forced to by people behind barricades with rocks and Molotov cocktails.

According to some accounts, one of the justifications for the project is that it would relieve traffic congestion around Taksim Square. Everyone who's been to the Square could probably agree that this would be desirable, so that might be where consultation could have begun. What alternatives exist that would calm or divert traffic without destroying the park? Perhaps there are none that are technically or economically feasible; if this conclusion were reached through consultation, then the selected approach might have enjoyed broad support, or at least have been tolerated as a thoughtful, rationally justified plan. Or, like the U.S. agencies who went into the Grand Canyon consultation intent on grinding up trout and came out of it agreeing to remove them alive, Erdoğan's faction might have come out of consultation with the Gezi Park people realizing that their own was not the only way to go. Maybe there are better ways to move traffic around Taksim Square, and even to achieve whatever economic benefits the shopping mall was/is intended to provide, without destroying Gezi. We'll never know, because the consultation that might have revealed such alternatives never took place.

Erdoğan is hardly unique. It's very human to become fixated on one's own particular solution to a problem, one's own particular means of achieving some benefit. Governments and their leaders may carry this fixation to extremes; after all, they're expected to solve problems, and make decisions. But nobody's decisions are always right; everybody's decision-making can benefit from being informed by thoughtful, meaningful consultation. To judge from Isaiah 1:18's admittedly cryptic lines, even God is humble enough to invite his children to reason together.

Glossary

ACHP: Advisory Council on Historic Preservation—the U.S. government agency that oversees federal agency project review under Section 106 of the National Historic Preservation Act (NHPA), and whose regulations, 36 CFR Part 800 (that is, title 36, part 800 of the Code of Federal Regulations) provide extensively for, and define, consultation.

Agency: In most if not all reviews conducted under laws like the National Environmental Policy Act (NEPA) and National Historic Preservation Act (NHPA), an agency of the United States government is a central player. They're usually the ones responsible for making sure the review happens, either because they're proposing the action or because they're considering assisting or permitting it. In other legal contexts (e.g., state, tribal, and local law in the U.S., and the laws of other nations), an agency may be part of some other sort of governmental body. Whatever the particulars, it's this sort of proponent or overseeing government entity that we usually mean when we use the term *agency.* If we mean a specific agency, we give it a real or apocryphal name. We often refer to *the responsible agency,* meaning the agency responsible for carrying out the environmental impact assessment (EIA) or cultural resource management (CRM) review; we do *not* mean to imply that such agencies always (or often) behave responsibly.

AIRFA: American Indian Religious Freedom Act (U.S.)

ARPA: Archaeological Resources Protection Act (U.S.)

BATNA: "Best alternative to a negotiated agreement"—a term introduced to consultation and negotiation practice by the original 1981 edition of the iconic *Getting to Yes* (Fisher, Uri & Patton 2011). The best you can get out of a situation if you don't negotiate an agreement with other interests.

CFR: Code of Federal Regulations, the compilation of official U.S. government regulations, usually referenced by "Title" and "Part" or "Section." "36 CFR 800," for example (referring to the NHPA Section 106 regulations), means Title 36, Part 800 of the Code, whereas "40 CFR 1500-1508" (referring to the NEPA Section 102(c) regulations) means Title 40, Sections 1500 through 1508 of the Code.

Consultant: A "consultant," says the Oxford English Dictionary Online, is "a person who provides expert advice professionally."[1] The authors, for instance, are consultants who provide ostensibly expert advice to people engaged in NHPA Section 106 review, EIA, and in Nissley's case, toxic materials remediation. A consultant, like any other human being, may become party to a consultation—that is, a consulting party (see below), but he or she is not automatically one; usually we find ourselves advising one or more such parties.

Consulting party: "Consulting party" is a commonly used term of art under NHPA Section 106; in that context it means someone—an individual, organization, agency, tribe—who consults about a project that's under review. We use the term more broadly here, but with a consistent meaning: it means anybody who consults or is consulted, or who ought to consult or be consulted, under any legal authority (or under no authority at all). A consultant (see above) may be a consulting party, but a consulting party is not necessarily a consultant.

CRM: Cultural Resource Management. This term of art is widely used in the United States, and increasingly in Australia, some African countries, and elsewhere, to refer to some set of laws, regulations, and practices designed to manage the cultural aspects of the environment and to control impacts on those aspects. The terms "cultural heritage management," or just "cultural heritage" are used elsewhere, and sometimes in the United States, to mean roughly the same thing. We use the term as King defined it in *A Companion to Cultural Resource Management* (King 2011:2):

> "Cultural resources" are all the aspects of the physical and supra-physical environment that human beings and their societies value for reasons having to do with culture. Included are culturally valued sites, buildings, and other places, plants and animals, atmospheric phenomena, sights and sounds, artifacts and other objects, documents, traditions, arts, crafts, ways of life, means of expression and

systems of belief. "Cultural Resource Management" means actions undertaken to manage such phenomena, or—importantly—to identify and manage the ways in which change affects or may affect them.

Many people and government agencies define the term more narrowly, and for purposes of this book the definition doesn't greatly matter; just understand that when we talk about consulting in "CRM" we're talking about consulting under laws, regulations, and practices dealing with some aspect or aspects of the cultural environment.

EA: Environmental Assessment. Rather confusingly, an EA is a kind of EIA (see below) performed in the United States under the National Environmental Policy Act (NEPA). Its purpose is to determine whether a project is likely to have a significant impact on the quality of the human environment, in which case an EIS (see below) must be performed.

EIA: Environmental Impact Assessment—a general term used internationally to embrace the laws, regulations, and practices involved in assessing the impacts of projects and proposals on the natural and cultural environments. In the United States EIA is performed under the authority of NEPA, state and tribal NEPA equivalents, and a number of related legal authorities. EIA is performed in other nations and in the context of international development under a range of other national and international laws, treaties, regional understandings, United Nations mandates, and funding agency rules.

EIS: Environmental Impact Statement—the formal, detailed analysis of environmental impacts that must be prepared in the United States under NEPA on any federal action likely to have significant impacts on the quality of the human environment.

FPIC: Free, prior, and informed consent—which the 2007 United Nations Declaration on the Rights of Indigenous Peoples says is supposed to be obtained from an indigenous group before some sort of change is imposed upon the group or its environment.

Government-to-government: "Government-to-government" consultation is obviously consultation that takes place between two governments. In the United States it is almost always understood to mean consultation between an agency or agencies of the U.S. government and the government of a federally recognized Indian tribe. Such consultation is naturally about matters of mutual interest—such as (though not necessarily) the potential impacts of a federal agency action on aspects of the environment that concern a tribe. Government-to-government consultation has certain special characteristics—notably that it must be carried out by or under the direct oversight of official government representatives—not technical staff or consultants. We touch on the complexities of government-to-government consultation at various points in this book.

Heritage: Generally, everyone's common inheritance—the natural environment, culture, history, the air, the water, the world. More narrowly, often thought of as "cultural heritage"—our legacy of values, beliefs, places, practices, places and things to which we ascribe cultural value. Often means the same as "cultural resource."

Historic preservation: The field(s) of practice that deal with buildings, sites, landscapes, and other places thought to have historical, architectural, archaeological, or cultural significance. Historic preservationists are usually trained in history, architecture, architectural history, and (sometimes under other names) archaeology, anthropology, cultural geography and planning. In the United States there is a large, rather complicated national historic preservation program.

Indian Tribe: In the United States, the term "Indian tribe" is legally defined in multiple laws and regulations to mean a "tribe, band, nation, or other organized group or community, including a native village, regional corporation or village corporation, as those terms are defined in section 3 of the Alaska Native Claims Settlement Act (43 U.S.C. 1602), which is recognized as eligible for the special programs and services provided by the United States to Indians because of their status as Indians" (c.f. 36 CFR § 800.14(m)). Such tribes are formally "recognized" or "acknowledged" by the U.S. government, and a directory of their governments is maintained by the Bureau of Indian Affairs.[2] Other tribes, although they are historically and culturally distinct, are not formally recognized by the U.S. government but nevertheless are called, and call themselves, Indian tribes. Essentially the same kinds of groups are called "First Nations" in Canada. In this book we use the term "Indian tribe" broadly to refer to any group made up of people of the Americas who self-identify as members of an indigenous community. Other indigenous people who live under the U.S. flag—notably Native Hawaiians but also including American Samoans, Chamorro people in the Mariana Islands, some native people of Puerto Rico and the Virgin Islands, and others—do not comprise Indian tribes but sometimes have special consultative rights under various laws and regulations.

Laws and Regulations: This is not a primer in the laws that require or encourage consultation, but we'll have occasion to refer to laws and regulations quite regularly. In the United States, a *law* is a statute enacted by some elected body—Congress, a state legislature, a local government council—while a *regulation* is a legally binding directive issued by some government entity like the Council on Environmental Quality or the Advisory Council on Historic Preservation, under the authority of one or more laws. Here are the U.S. laws and regulations we refer to often:

- The *National Environmental Policy Act (NEPA)*, particularly Section 102(C), which we usually refer to by its acronym;
- The *National Historic Preservation Act (NHPA)*, notably Sections 106 and 110; our convention is to call them *NHPA Section 106* and *NHPA Section 110*;
- The *Endangered Species Act (ESA)*, which we usually spell out;
- The *Native American Graves Protection and Repatriation Act* (NAGPRA), referred to by its acronym;
- The *Archaeological Resources Protection Act* (ARPA), referred to by its acronym;
- The *NHPA Section 106 regulations* (36 CFR Part 800), issued by the *Advisory Council on Historic Preservation (ACHP)*;
- The *NEPA regulations* (40 CFR Part 1500-1508), issued by the *Council on Environmental Quality (CEQ)*; and
- The ARPA uniform regulations issued by U.S. Department of Interior (43 CFR Part 7).

MOA: Memorandum of Agreement—under Section 106 of the U.S. NHPA, the document usually produced through consultation specifying how the adverse effects of a project on historic places will be dealt with.

NAGPRA: Native American Graves Protection and Repatriation Act (U.S.)

NEPA: National Environmental Policy Act (U.S.)

NHPA: National Historic Preservation Act (U.S.)

Project: When we use the term "project," we're referring to whatever kind of project is subjected to review under the EIA and CRM laws and regulations. Examples from our own experience over the last few years include but are not limited to:

- Development of wind and solar energy projects;
- Redevelopment of medical facilities for military veterans;
- Development of mines and quarries;
- Management of wild horses and burros;
- Remediation of toxic waste sites;
- Construction of highway interchanges, railroads, and multimodal transit facilities; and
- Disposal of government facilities no longer needed for their original purposes.

Proponent: The sponsor of a proposed project (see "sponsor or proponent" below).

Review: Most times when we use the word "review," we mean the review of a proposed project's effects on the environment, or some aspect of the environment, under one or more laws or regulations.

Section 106: Refers to Section 106 of NHPA, which requires U.S. federal agencies to take into account the effect of their actions on historic places and afford the Advisory Council on Historic Preservation (ACHP) a reasonable opportunity to comment. The ACHP's regulations, at 36 CFR Part 800, include consultation requirements.

Sponsor or Proponent: The sponsor or proponent of a project is, of course, the entity that proposes to make it happen—often a government agency, sometimes a corporation or other business entity, occasionally an individual.

TEK: Traditional ecological or environmental knowledge—the knowledge of the environment of a place or region possessed by an indigenous or other traditional community.

You: Exactly who we mean when we use the word "you"—as we do a great deal—depends on the context in which we use it. Often we're talking to the person or people who are responsible for consulting on behalf of a project sponsor or an oversight agency. In some cases we're talking to those consulting on behalf of some other stakeholder—an Indian tribe or other indigenous group, an affected community, a citizens' group, a local government, property owners, or whoever else may need and want to consult. We try to be clear in each case we use the term just who we mean by "you."

Two Invitations to Consult

A U.S. Bureau of Land Management Letter

Here is the text of a real letter sent out in 2012 by a state office of the U.S. Department of the Interior, Bureau of Land Management (BLM); it happens to be addressed to Indian tribes in a western U.S. state, but with a few minor modifications could have been sent to anyone. Names have been deleted; our intent is not to criticize individuals, but to give an example of the kind of letter that government agencies all too often send out to "initiate consultation" when they actually intend to do no such thing.

Chairman XXX

XXX Tribe

Dear Chairman XXX:

The Bureau of Land Management (BLM) recognizes that the United States has a unique legal and political relationship with Indian tribal governments, established through and confirmed by the Constitution of the United States treaties, statutes, executive orders, and judicial decisions. In recognition of that special relationship, pursuant to Executive Order 13175 of November 6, 2000, we are charged with engaging in regular and meaningful consultation and collaboration with Tribal officials in the development of Federal policies that have Tribal implications, and are responsible for strengthening the government-to-government relationship between the United States and Indian Tribes.

Comment: Does the Chairman need to be informed of all this? Why? Do he and his colleagues not know these fundamental facts? Or is the idea to demonstrate that BLM knows them?

It is with this understanding that the BLM invites you to consult with us as we revise the current Anystate Protocol that prescribes the manner in which the BLM and the State Historic Preservation Officer (SHPO) comply with Section 106 of the National Historic Preservation Act (NHPA) by cooperatively implementing the recently revised National Programmatic Agreement (NPA) in Anystate.

Comment: Quite a mouthful, and it's still not clear what BLM is asking.

In carrying out its responsibilities specific to the NHPA, the BLM executed a NPA in February of 2012 with the Advisory Council on Historic Preservation (ACHP) and the National Conference of State Historic Preservation Officers (NCSHPO) to help guide the BLM's planning and decision making as it affects historic properties as defined in the NHPA. The State Protocol Agreement is being revised pursuant to provisions of the NPA and revises the provisions of the State Protocol Agreement (Protocol) between the Anystate State Director of the BLM and the Anystate State Historic Preservation Officer (SHPO), executed on October 15, 2007.

Comment: "*Being* revised." So here, buried in convoluted and acronym-laden text, the Chairman may notice that revision of the Protocol is already underway; he is *not* being consulted early in its development, but only after revisions have been undertaken. It gets worse.

The Protocol establishes the procedures that govern the interaction between the BLM and the SHPO under the NPA. The Protocol is intended to ensure that the BLM organizes its programs to operate efficiently and effectively in accordance with the intent and requirements of the NHPA and that the BLM integrates its historic preservation planning and management decisions with other policy and program requirements.

Comment: Abstract, soothing language: the Chairman is being asked to believe that BLM's intent is to do good.

The Protocol streamlines the NHPA Section 106 (Section 106) process by eliminating case-by-case consultation with the SHPO on undertakings that culminate in "no historic properties affected" (36 CFR 800.4(d)(1)) and "no adverse effect" findings (36 CFR 800.5(b)). The Protocol also requires development and management of a Historic Preservation Program (Section 110 of the NHPA) and implementation of the Program by each Field Office in partial exchange for relief from the case-by-case procedural requirements of 36 CFR 800.

Comment: So BLM already knows what the Protocol is going to do, and how it's going to do it. It's going to "streamline" the NHPA Section 106 process, and it's going to do it by eliminating case by case SHPO consultation on cases where certain "findings" are made. These findings are made by BLM, and what BLM is in fact proposing—though the letter obscures it—is to do it unilaterally. For practical purposes, the effect of this bit of "streamlining" will be to allow BLM to make NHPA Section 106 findings without talking to *anyone* on the outside, unless the BLM itself determines that there will be adverse effects on historic properties, as it defines them. A beautifully closed system.

The current Protocol (enclosed) is being revised to reflect existing authorities and new policy. Authorities for managing cultural resources and programs of historic preservation exist under the National Environmental Policy Act (NEPA, Pub. L. 91-190), the Federal Lands Policy and Management Act (FLPMA, Pub. L. 91-579), the Archaeological Resources Protection Act (ARPA, 16 USC 470), the Native American Graves Protection and Repatriation Act (NAGPRA, 25 USC 3001), the Historic Sites Act of 1935 (Pub. L. 73-

292), the Antiquities Act of 1906 (16 USC 431-433), the American Indian Religious Freedom Act (AIRFA, Pub. L. 95-341), Executive Order 13007 ("Sacred Sites," 61 FR 105), Consultation and Coordination with Indian Tribal Governments (Executive Order 13175), the Department of the Interior Policy on Consultation with Indian Tribes (Secretarial Order No. 3317), Memorandum for the Heads of Executive Departments and Agencies on Tribal Consultation (75 FR 78709), and the National Historic Preservation Act of 1966 as amended (NHPA, Pub. L. 89-665).

Comment: This blizzard of citations serves no purpose other than to swamp the reader in its verbiage, and perhaps to convey the impression that there is legal authority for the Protocol.

Although consultation has no deadline, a response within 15 days indicating your interest in participating in the revision of the Protocol will be most helpful. If you would like to participate in the revision of the Protocol, please send written comments to YYYYY at the address above, by E-mail to YYYY@ZZZZ, or at (XXX) XXX-XXXX.

Sincerely,

State Director

Comment: So finally, at the very end of the letter, BLM actually asks the Chairman to consult—sort of. But what is he being asked to do? Just advise the BLM's designated representative that his Tribe wants to consult? Or to provide comments? If so, on what should he comment? BLM doesn't tell him, but it does strongly hint that he'd better do it within fifteen days.

How would you react if you received a letter like the above? If you needed to send a letter of this kind, how would you improve on this example?

A U.S. Department of Veterans Affairs Letter

Here is another real letter, this one inviting Indian Tribes to participate in consultation about the fate of a building associated with a historic Indian school. Again, names have been deleted.

> Dear Chairman XXX
>
> As you know, the Department of Veterans Affairs (VA) manages the Veterans Medical Center at YYYY, which includes the site of the former YYYY Indian School. The School is eligible for inclusion in the National Register of Historic Places. The Center's Building N, part of the School, is in a deteriorating condition and, in the opinion of VA's engineers, is beyond rehabilitation and re-use. Accordingly, VA proposes to demolish it.
>
> At various times over the last several years, VA has initiated review of this proposal under Section 106 of the National Historic Preservation Act, but for one reason or another, the process has never been completed. We are now scheduling a meeting at YYYY among VA, the State Historic Preservation Officer (SHPO) and the Advisory Council on Historic Preservation (ACHP) to discuss the potential demolition of Building N, and determine whether we can reach a memorandum of agreement in accordance with the ACHP's Section 106 regulations. I am writing to invite you to participate in this meeting, and in general consultation under Section 106, as well as to solicit any thoughts or suggestions you may have about Building N or the Indian School in general.
>
> The meeting is tentatively scheduled for March 25. Please let me know if you would like to participate. I look forward to hearing from you.

How does this letter differ from the BLM example? Note that in this case, despite years of on-again, off-again communication about the building, which had built up a considerable level of frustration among the tribes and with the SHPO, the meeting resulted in a Memorandum of Agreement among the agency, SHPO, ACHP, and several tribes, under which the building was documented and demolished with tribal oversight.

The Colorado River Fish Management Memorandum of Agreement

MEMORANDUM OF AGREEMENT
Non-Native Fish Control in the Colorado River Below Glen Canyon Dam

WHEREAS the Bureau of Reclamation (Reclamation), U.S. Department of the Interior (DOI), manages the release of water out of Glen Canyon Dam down the Colorado River through the Glen Canyon, Marble Canyon, and Grand Canyon in Arizona (Canyons), in accordance with the Colorado River Storage Project Act of 1956 (CRSPA), the Grand Canyon Protection Act (GCPA), and other authorities collectively known as the "Law of the River;" and

Whereas, Reclamation consulted with the U.S. Fish and Wildlife Service (FWS) under § 7 of the Endangered Species Act of 1973, as amended, on the effect on listed species on the continued operation of Glen Canyon Dam under modified low fluctuating flows with the inclusion of a protocol for high-flow experimental releases and non-native fish control for the ten-year period, 2011-2020; and

Whereas, as a result of those consultations, in December 2011 the FWS issued a biological opinion that described various actions and conservation measures, including non-native fish control in the Colorado River downstream from Glen Canyon Dam, to which Reclamation is committed; and

Claudia Nissley and Thomas F. King, "The Colorado River Fish Management Memorandum of Agreement" in *Consultation and Cultural Heritage: Let Us Reason Together,* pp. 147-155. © 2014 Left Coast Press, Inc. All rights reserved.

Note: These clauses provide background on the undertaking addressed in the MOA.

Whereas, Reclamation now has consulted with various parties under § 106 of the National Historic Preservation Act of 1966 (NHPA), as amended, to assess the effects on historic properties from the undertaking, non-native fish control as described in the FWS's biological opinion; and

Whereas, the National Park Service (NPS), U.S. Department of the Interior, protects and manages units of the national park system within Grand Canyon National Park (GRCA) and Glen Canyon National Recreation Area (GLCA), including the lands and waters in the Canyons, and is responsible for identifying, managing, and preserving historic properties within GRCA and GLCA pursuant to §§ 110 and 106 of the National Historic Preservation Act of 1966, as amended (NHPA); and

Whereas, Reclamation and the NPS recognize that Reclamation is the lead federal agency for purposes of compliance with § 106 of the NHPA for the undertaking, non-native fish control, described in this agreement; and

Whereas, Western Area Power Administration, under the Act of Congress approved August 4, 1977 (91 Stat. 565) is responsible for marketing power and energy and transmitting electric power generated at the facilities of the Colorado River Storage Project, including Glen Canyon Dam, to preference customers in various states, and also has responsibility for managing the Upper Colorado River Basin Fund which funds various work related to historic properties protection within the area of potential effects (APE), and is authorized as part of the Colorado River Storage Project Act of 1956 (70 Stat. 105), consistent with sound business principles to ensure repayment of Colorado River Storage Project construction and operation expenses to the United States Treasury (36 CFR 800.2(c)(5)); and

Note: These clauses provide background on the undertaking addressed in the MOA.

Whereas, the APE for the proposed undertaking is the Colorado River between Lees Ferry and Lava Chuar Rapid in Glen Canyon National Recreation Area and Grand Canyon National Park; and

Note: "APE" means "area of potential effects," a term of art under NHPA Section 106; it refers to the area or areas where a federal action, if carried forward, may have effects on historic places.

Whereas, the Hopi Tribe, the Hualapai Tribe, the Kaibab Band of the Paiute Indians, the Navajo Nation, the Paiute Indian Tribe of Utah for Shivwits Band, and the Pueblo of Zuni (collectively "the Tribes") are federally recognized Indian tribes; and

Whereas, the Tribes have advised Reclamation that they attach religious or cultural significance to historic properties located within the Canyons, including the entire Grand Canyon, and also regard the Canyons including the Colorado River as constituting a Traditional Cultural Property (TCP) eligible for the National Register of Historic Places (National Register); and

Whereas, Reclamation, in consultation with NPS and the Tribes, has determined that the Colorado River and the Canyons are eligible for the National Register as a TCP, and the Arizona State Historic Preservation Officer (SHPO) and NPS have concurred in so regarding them; and

Note: The above clause builds on the previous one, and is pivotal in documenting why the case was considered under NHPA Section 106.

Whereas, the Pueblo of Zuni (Zuni) in Tribal Council Resolution M70-2010-C086 and other representations, has advised Reclamation that the lethal removal of fish is offensive to Zuni cultural and spiritual values and an act of desecration, and specifically counterproductive to Zuni's efforts, grounded deeply in Zuni traditional and cultural values, to ensure harmony and prosperity of all life; and

Whereas, other Tribes have supported Zuni in its expression of concern; and

Whereas, Reclamation has accordingly determined that lethal removal of non-native fish would constitute an adverse effect on the historic and cultural character and use of the canyons; and

Note: This represents the federal government's acknowledgement that its action had adverse effects that needed to be addressed.

Whereas, Reclamation therefore revised its undertaking to avoid adverse effects to cultural resources by committing to live removal of non-native fish when conducting non-native fish removal is necessary to comply with the ESA; and

Note: This clause is cosmetic, inserted by Reclamation late in the drafting process. In fact, of course, the tribes, SHPO and other parties labored long and hard to prevail on Reclamation to abandon the lethal removal of fish; indeed this was the major reason the consultation took place. Such face-saving provisions are not uncommonly included in agreements, and may be necessary to getting them signed.

Whereas, pursuant to Section 106 of the NHPA and its implementing regulations (36 CFR Part 800), Reclamation has consulted with all parties who have expressed an interest in the protection of historic properties related to the proposed undertaking, specifically NPS, the Tribes, the Advisory Council on Historic Preservation (ACHP), the Arizona SHPO, the Bureau of Indian Affairs, the U.S. Fish and Wildlife Service, Western Area Power Administration, Colorado River Energy Distributors' Association, and the Grand Canyon Monitoring and Research Center, and invited these parties to sign or concur in this memorandum of agreement (MOA) pursuant to 36 CFR § 800.6(c); and

Whereas, Reclamation has consulted with the public through the National Environmental Policy Act process; and

Note: The above clause seems like something of a throw-away, but in fact the NEPA process did serve to alert interested parties, who could then ask to be consulted.

> Whereas, in accordance with 36 C.F.R. § 800.6(a)(1), Reclamation has notified the Advisory Council on Historic Preservation (ACHP) of its adverse effect determination providing the specified documentation, and the ACHP has chosen to be a signatory; and
>
> Whereas, Reclamation has invited the ACHP to participate in consultation, and the ACHP has participated to seek ways to avoid, minimize, or mitigate adverse effects to historic properties resulting from the undertaking and to develop this memorandum of agreement (MOA);
>
> NOW, THEREFORE, the signatories agree that should Reclamation decide to proceed with actions that may lead to non-native fish removal, Reclamation will ensure that the following measures are implemented to resolve the adverse effects of such removal on historic properties.

Note: The above is certainly a large collection of "whereas" clauses to wade through before getting to the stipulations that actually say what's been agreed to, but in this case it would have been difficult to cut them down much.

Stipulations

> In consultation and collaboration with all parties to this MOA, Reclamation shall ensure the following stipulations are carried out:
>
> 1. Reclamation, to the maximum extent practicable, will remove non-native fish alive, thereby avoiding adverse effects to the Colorado River and the Canyons and address the concerns raised by the Tribes, in accordance with the following:

a. Reclamation, in removing non-native fishes in the Colorado River between Lees Ferry (river mile 0) and Lava Chuar Creek (river mile 65), will conduct up to 10 trips annually in the Paria River to Badger Creek area and up to 6 trips annually near the Little Colorado River confluence between Kwagunt Rapid to Lava Chuar Creek. These removals will only be undertaken if the best available science indicates that these non-native fish are posing a threat to endangered fish species.

b. Reclamation will notify the Tribes and other consulting parties of its intention to conduct live removal as soon as possible but at a minimum 30 days in advance.

c. The Tribes may, if they so choose, participate in non-native fish control efforts if they occur, in order to assure that they are being conducted appropriately with regard to tribal concerns.

d. Prior to each live removal effort that occurs, Reclamation will coordinate with Tribes and other consulting parties on the need to conduct removal and relocation sites for live non-native fish.

Note: This is the key stipulation: live removal in consultation with the tribes. It contains some weasel-words like "to the maximum extent practicable," which it would have been desirable to avoid.

2. Should live removal prove infeasible, Reclamation will reconsult with the Tribes and other consulting parties to determine acceptable mitigation for adverse effects of the action.

3. In any event, Reclamation shall abide by the terms of the agreement between Reclamation and the Navajo Nation executed on DATE entitled "Agreement Between the Bureau of Reclamation and the Navajo Nation to Avoid Adverse Impacts —Non-Native Fish Control in the Colorado River below Glen Canyon Dam".

Note: This separate and prior agreement (someone forgot to include the date) specified where in the river fish removal could occur.

4. Resolving Objections:

   a. Should any party to this MOA object in writing or electronically to Reclamation regarding any action carried out or proposed with respect to non-native fish control or implementation of this MOA, Reclamation will consult with the objecting party to resolve the objection. If after initiating such consultation Reclamation determines that the objection cannot be resolved through consultation, Reclamation will forward all documentation relevant to the objection to the ACHP, including Reclamation's proposed response to the objection.

   b. Within 30 days after receipt of all pertinent documentation, the ACHP will exercise one of the following options:

      I. Advise Reclamation that the ACHP concurs in Reclamation's proposed response to the objection, whereupon Reclamation will respond to the objection accordingly;

      II. Provide Reclamation with recommendations, which Reclamation will take into account in reaching a final decision regarding its response to the objection; or

      II. Notify Reclamation that the objection will be referred for comment pursuant to 36 CFR 800.7(a)(4), and proceed to refer the objection and comment. Reclamation will take the resulting comment into account in accordance with 36 CFR 800.7(c)(4) and Section 110(l) of NHPA.

   c. Should the ACHP not exercise one of the above options within 30 days after receipt of all pertinent documentation, Reclamation may assume the ACHP's concurrence in its proposed response to the objection.

    d.   Reclamation will take into account any ACHP recommendation or comment provided in accordance with this stipulation with reference only to the subject of the objection; Reclamation's responsibility to carry out all actions under this MOA that are not the subjects of the objection will remain unchanged.

    e.   At any time during implementation of the measures stipulated in this MOA, should an objection pertaining to this MOA or the effect of non-native fish control on historic properties be raised by a member of the public, Reclamation will notify the parties to this MOA and take the objection into account, consulting with the objector and, should the objector so request, with any of the parties to this MOA to resolve the objection.

5.   Amendments: This MOA may only be amended by mutual written consent of the signatories. Amendments shall not be effective until approved by all signatories.

6.   Termination: Any signatory may terminate this agreement in accordance with 36 C.F.R. § 800.6(c)(8) and by providing the other signatories with 60 days advance written notice of its intention to do so. If any signatory provides the other signatories with notice of its intention to terminate this agreement, then the signatories agree to meet to discuss the issues that prompted the notice and to try to resolve them through further consultation or by amending this agreement. In order to be considered a "signatory" for purposes of this termination provision, a party must sign this agreement within 60 days after the last date when Reclamation, the NPS, the SHPO, or the ACHP signs the agreement.

    a.   Notwithstanding any of the above, this MOA will expire eleven (11) years after the date of its execution by Reclamation, unless the signatories hereto, in consultation with the other parties and such others as may have become involved in implementation of this MOA, agree in writing to extend its terms.

7. Anti-Deficiency Act: Reclamation's obligations under this MOA are subject to the availability of appropriated funds, and the stipulations of this MOA are subject to the provisions of the Anti-Deficiency Act. Reclamation will make reasonable and good faith efforts to secure the necessary funds to implement this MOA in its entirety. If compliance with the Anti-Deficiency Act alters or impairs Reclamation's ability to implement the stipulations of this agreement, Reclamation will consult in accordance with the amendment and termination procedures found at 5 and 6 above.

Note: The above are standard-language stipulations used in NHPA Section 106 agreements; they are important to ensure that implementation is administered in accordance with agreed-upon norms.

Execution and implementation of this MOA evidences that Reclamation has afforded the SHPO and ACHP a reasonable opportunity to comment on the effects of nonnative fish control on historic properties. Execution and compliance with this MOA fulfills Reclamation's Section 106 responsibilities regarding this undertaking.

SIGNATORIES:

Note: The MOA was signed by representatives of the Bureau of Reclamation, the National Park Service, the Advisory Council on Historic Preservation, the Arizona State Historic Preservation Office, the Pueblo of Zuni, the Hopi Tribe, the Hualapai Tribe, the Navajo Nation, the Kaibab Band of Paiute Indians, the Paiute Indian Tribe of Utah (for the Shivwits Paiute Tribe), and the Western Area Power Administration, with concurrence by the Bureau of Indian Affairs, the Colorado River Energy Distributors Association, the U.S. Fish and Wildlife Service, and the U.S. Geological Survey.

Chapter 3

1. *Pueblo of Sandia v. United States,* 50 F.3d 856 (10th Cir. 1995)

2. *Comanche Nation v. United States,* No CIV-08-849-D, 2008 WI. 4426621 (W.D. Okla. Sep 23, 2008)

3. Quechan Tribe of the Fort Yuma Reservation v. U.S. Department of the Interior, US Dist. Ct. S. Dist. CA 2010

4. Three years later, in an identically titled case involving a wind energy project, the same court found for the government; see *Quechan Tribe of the Ft. Yuma Reservation v. U.S. Department of the Interior,* US Dist. Ct. S. Dist. CA 2013. We are still puzzling over this opinion; King, who worked on another tribe's critique of the project but did not take part in the litigation, thinks the Quechan's attorneys simply failed to make their case.

5. Other cases very probably include the 2013 Quechan case, but in that case they got away with it.

6. You have every right, if, that is, you're a citizen in a representative democracy, and of course we're speaking theoretically here; even in a democracy, governments and corporations have plenty of ways to suppress theoretical rights.

Chapter 4

1. "A camel is a horse designed by a committee." Popular aphorism.

2. Executive Order 12898 on Environmental Justice (Clinton 1994)

3. 1786, "To A Louise" www.robertburns.org/works/97.shtml (Accessed 7 July 2013)

4. Examples of such organizations are the International Association of Facilitators, www.iaf-world.org/index.aspx, and the Association for Conflict Resolution, www.acrnet.org/.

Chapter 5

1. For the text of these standards, see www.nps.gov/history/hdp/ (Accessed 7 July 2013).

2. For an example of historical views that can be downloaded, see www.historypin .com/ (Accessed 20 July 2013).

3. For more information on this controversy, see www.justice.gov/usao/mt/press releases/20130129164041.html (Accessed 7 July 2012). Monitoring is seldom a practical way to control impacts on cultural sites of any kind, but it can be an easy thing to agree to.

4. Text for this NRHP eligibility criterion may be found in 36 CFR § 60.4(d).

5. *Henry VI,* Part 2, shakespeare.mit.edu/2henryvi/full.html (Accessed 20 July 2013)

6. 36 CFR 800.11(a)

7. 36 CFR 800.11(e)(6), see also 36 CFR 800.11(g)(3)

Chapter 6

1. Innes and Booher (2010 and personal communication 2013) refer to this approach as the "DEAD" model—"Decide, Educate, Announce, Defend."

2. Alternatively the agency may be required to consult with the Tribal Historic Preservation Officer (THPO) on tribal lands, and with federally recognized tribes where places of cultural or spiritual significance to them may be involved, but these are somewhat special cases.

3. U.S. Department of State, Announcement of U.S. Support for the United Nations Declaration on the Rights of Indigenous Peoples, 12 January 2011, state.gov/s/srgia/154553 .htm

4. Bryer during oral arguments in *Koons Buick Pontiac GMC Inc. v. Nigh,* No. 04-377, 2004, a case that turned on interpretation of the word "subparagraph." See www.oyez.org/cases/2000-2009/2004/2004_03_377#sort=vote (Accessed 9 July 2013).

5. For information on adaptive management, see www.resalliance.org/index.php/ adaptive_management (Accessed 10 August 2013).

6. The ACHP does not always tell agencies that they *have* done wrong; it may say that an agency has done just fine. However, the presence of historic preservation experts and advocates on the Council, as specified in the law, makes it tend to lean in the direction of promoting preservation.

Chapter 7

1. The meeting was also organized to further another consultation on the overall management of water releases out of the dam and their effects on the cultural environment.

Appendix 1

1. oxforddictionaries.com/definition/english/consultant?q=consultant (Accessed 1 Sept 2013)
2. For this directory, see www.bia.gov/WhoWeAre/BIA/OIS/TribalGovernment-Services/TribalDirectory/ (Accessed 6 July 2013).References

REFERENCES

Publications Cited

ABD (African Development Bank, Environment and Sustainable Development Unit)

2001 *Handbook on Stakeholder Consultation and Participation in ABD Operations* www.afdb.org/fileadmin/uploads/afdb/Documents/Policy-Documents/Handbook%20on%20Stakeholder%20Consultaion.pdf (Accessed 6 July 2013).

Alonzo, Monica

2012 Desecration: Unearthed Native Burial Site Causes Uproar. Phoenix, AZ, *Phoenix New Times,* November 29, www.phoenixnewtimes.com/2012-11-29/news/desecration-unearthed-native-burial-site-causes-uproar/ (Accessed 6 July 2013).

Bejerle, Thomas C.

2002 *Democracy in Practice: Public Participation in Environmental Decisions.* Oxford, Routledge.

CEAA (Canadian Environmental Assessment Agency)

2012 *Public Participation,* www.ceaa-acee.gc.ca/default. asp?lang=En&n=8A52D8E4-1 (Accessed 5 July 2013).

Clinton, President William J.

1994 *Federal Actions to Address Environmental Justice in Minority Populations and Low Income Populations.* Executive Order 12898, www.epa.gov/fedrgstr/eo/eo12898.pdf (Accessed 7 July 2013).

Cohen, Raymond

1997 *Negotiating Across Cultures: International Communication in an Interdependent World* (Revised Edition). Washington DC, Institute of Peace Press.

Dietz, Thomas & Paul C. Stern, Eds.
2008 *Public Participation in Environmental Assessment and Decision Making.* Washington D.C., National Academies Press.

Dorochoff, Nicholas
2007 *Negotiation Basics for Cultural Resource Managers.* Walnut Creek, CA, Left Coast Press, Inc.

Environmental Agency (England and Wales)
2010 *Working Together: Your Role in Our Environmental Permitting.* www. environment-agency.gov.uk/static/documents/Business/Working_together_PPS_v2.0.pdf (Accessed July 5, 2013).

EPA (Environmental Protection Agency, U.S.)
2000 *Public Participation Guide,* www.epa.gov/international/public-participation-guide/ (Accessed 5 July 2013).

Fischer, Frank
2000 *Citizens, Experts, and the Environment: The Politics of Local Knowledge.* Durham, NC, Duke University Press.

Fisher, Roger, William Ury & Bruce Patton
2011 *Getting to Yes: Negotiating Agreement Without Giving In,* Revised Edition. New York, Penguin Press.

Fuller, Reba
2011 Consultation in Cultural Resource Management: An Indigenous Perspective. Chapter 21 in *Companion to Cultural Resource Management,* T.F. King, ed., Oxford, Wiley-Blackwell: 373-84.

Hall, Edward T.
1976 *Beyond Culture.* New York, Anchor Books.

Hansen, Joyce & Gary McGowan
1998 *Breaking Ground, Breaking Silence: The Story of New York's African Burial Ground.* New York, Henry Holt & Co.

Innes, Judith E. & David E. Booher
2004 Reframing Public Participation: Strategies for the 21st Century. *Planning Theory and Practice* 5(4):419-36.
2010 *Planning with Complexity: An Introduction to Collaborative Rationality for Public Policy.* New York, Routledge.

Kaner, Sam, Michael Doyle, Lenny Lind, Catherine Toldi, Sarah Fisk & Duane Berger
2007 *Facilitator's Guide to Participatory Decision-Making.* New York, Jossey-Bass.

Kaufman, Ned

2009   *Race, Place, and Story: Essays on the Past and Future of Historic Preserva-*
        tion. New York, Routledge.

King, Thomas F.

2003   *Places That Count: Traditional Cultural Properties in Cultural Resource*
        Management. Lanham, MD, Altamira Press.

2004   *Federal Planning and Historic Places: The Section 106 Process.* Lanham,
        MD, Altamira Press.

2007   *Saving Places That Matter: A Citizen's Guide to the National Historic Pres-*
        ervation Act. Walnut Creek, CA, Left Coast Press, Inc.

2009   *Our Unprotected Heritage: Whitewashing the Destruction of our Cultural*
        and Natural Environment. Walnut Creek, CA, Left Coast Press, Inc.

2010   What Burdens Religion? Musings on Two Recent Cases Interpreting
        the Religious Freedom Restoration Act. *Great Plains Natural Resources*
        Journal 13:1-11, Vermillion, SD, University of South Dakota.

2011   *Companion to Cultural Resource Management.* (Editor) Oxford, Wiley-Black-
        well.

2013   *Cultural Resource Laws and Practice* (4th Edition). Lanham, MD, Altamira
        Press.

MacMillan, Leslie

2012   *Bison Bones, a Backhoe, and a Crow Curse.* Outside Online, 11/9/12,
        www.outsideonline.com/adventure-travel/north-america/united-states/
        montana/Bison-Bones-a-Backhoe-and-a-Crow-Curse.html?page=all
        (Accessed 7 July 2013).

Mayo, Tony

2010   *How to Conduct a "Customer Listening Session."* mayogenuine.com/blog/
        how-to-conduct-a-customer-listening-session/ (Accessed 7 July 2013).

McCarthy, John P.

1996   Who Owns These Bones? Descendent Communities and Partnerships in
        the Excavation and Analysis of Historic Cemetery Sites in New York and
        Philadelphia. *Public Archaeology Review* 4(2):3-11.

2008   The Archaeology of Community Identity in the Past and Remembrance
        in the Present. *American Nineteenth Century History* 9(3):305-14.

Menzies, Charles R.

2006   *Traditional Ecological Knowledge and Natural Resource Management.*
        Lincoln, NE, University of Nebraska Press.

Nesper, Larry, Anna Willow & T. F. King

2002   *The Mushgigagamongsebe District: A Traditional Cultural Landscape of the Sokaogon Ojibwe Community.* Kindle publication—www.amazon.com/ Mushgigamongsebe-District-Traditional-Landscape-ebook/dp/B008A-K7AJQ/ref=la_B001IU2RWK_1_21?s=books&ie=UTF8&qid=13797725 82&sr=1-21

Nissley, Claudia

2011   Consultation and Negotiation in Cultural Resource Management. Chapter 25 in T.F. King, ed., *Companion to Cultural Resource Management,* Oxford, Wiley-Blackwell: 439-53.

NRC (National Research Council, U.S.)

2008   *Public Participation in Environmental Assessment and Decision Making.* Washington, D.C., The National Academies Press.

Parker, Patricia & Thomas F. King

1987   "Intercultural Mediation at Truk International Airport." In *Anthropological Praxis: Translating Knowledge Into Action.* R.W. Wulff and S.J. Fiske, eds., Washington Association of Professional Anthropologists, Boulder, CO, Westview Press.

Pflugh, Kerry Kirk & Suzanne Shannon

1991   *Alternatives to Public Hearings that Meet Regulatory Requirements: A Workbook for an Improved Procedure.* Trenton, NJ, New Jersey Department of Environmental Protection, Division of Science and Research, Risk Communication Unit and Office of Public Participation.

Rio Tinto

2011   *Why Cultural Heritage Matters: A Resource Guide for Integrating Cultural Heritage Management into Communities Work at Rio Tinto.* www.riotinto .com/documents/ReportsPublications/Rio_Tinto_Cultural_Heritage_ Guide.pdf (Accessed 15 July 2013).

SCBD (Secretariat of the Convention on Biological Diversity)

2004   *Akwé Kon Voluntary Guidelines for the Conduct of Cultural, Environmental and Social Impact Assessments Regarding Developments Proposed to Take Place on, or Which are Likely to Impact on, Sacred Sites and on Lands and Waters Traditionally Occupied or Used by Indigenous and Local Communities.* www. cbd.int/doc/publications/akwe-brochure-en.pdf (Accessed 10 July 2013).

SEA Info.Net

n.d.   *Strategic Environmental Assessment Information Service.* www.sea-info. net/ (Accessed 5 July 2013).

Solvit Dispute Resolution

2010   Chetwynd, Taseko, and the Duty to Consult: Meaningful Interest-Based Dialogue. solvitdisputeresolution.com/2010/11/16/chetwynd-taseko-and-the-duty-to-consult-meaningful-interest-based-dialogue/ (Accessed 18 July 2013).

United Nations

2007   *Declaration on the Rights of Indigenous Peoples.* www.un.org/esa/socdev/unpfii/documents/DRIPS_en.pdf (Accessed 6 July 2013).

Video Arts

1975   *Decisions, Decisions: Making and Acting On Decisions.* www.videoarts.com/leadership/decisions-decisions/ (Accessed 5 July 2013).

Winter, Joseph C.

1993   Navajo Sacred Sites and the Transwestern Pipeline Expansion Project. In *Papers from the Third, Fourth, and Sixth Navajo Studies Conference,* Window Rock, AZ, Navajo Nation Historic Preservation Department: 65-109.

Laws Cited

American Indian Religious Freedom Act (AIRFA), 42 U.S.C. §§ 1996 & 1996a, www.cr.nps.gov/local-law/fhpl_IndianRelFreAct.pdf (Accessed 8 July 2013).

Archaeological Resources Protection Act (ARPA), 16 U.S.C. §§ 469aa-mm, www.cr.nps.gov/local-law/fhpl_archrsrcsprot.pdf (Accessed 8 July 2013).

Clean Water Act (CWA), 33 U.S.C. §§ 1251-1387, www.waterboards.ca.gov/laws_regulations/docs/fedwaterpollutioncontrolact.pdf (Accessed 8 July 2013).

Federal Records Act (FRA), 5 U.S.C. Chap. 5; 18 U.S.C. Chap's. 101, 121; 31 U.S.C. Chap. 11; 40 U.S.C. Chap. 25; 44. U.S.C. Chap's. 21, 29, 31, 33, 35, www.archives.gov/records-mgmt/laws/ (Accessed 8 July 2013).

Native American Graves Protection and Repatriation Act (NAGPRA), 25 U.S.C. § 3001 et seq., www.nps.gov/nagpra/mandates/25usc3001etseq.htm (Accessed 8 July 2013).

National Environmental Policy Act (NEPA), 42 U.S.C. §§ 4321-75, ceq.hss.doe.gov/nepa/regs/nepa/nepaeqia.htm (Accessed 8 July 2013).

National Historic Preservation Act (NHPA), 16 U.S.C. § 470 et seq., www.nps.gov/history/local-law/nhpa1966.htm (Accessed 8 July 2013).

Religious Freedom Restoration Act (RFRA), 42 U.S.C. § 21B, www.law.cornell.edu/uscode/text/42/chapter-21B (Accessed 8 July 2013).

Regulations Cited

National Register of Historic Places: 36 CFR Part 60, cfr.regstoday.com/36cfr.aspx (Accessed 8 July 2013).

NHPA Section 106 review: 36 CFR Part 800, www.achp.gov/regs-rev04.pdf (Accessed 8 July 2013).

NEPA Section 102(c) regulations: 40 CFR Part 1500-1508, ceq.hss.doe.gov/ceq_regulations/Council_on_Environmental_Quality_Regulations.pdf (Accessed 8 July 2013).

NAGPRA regulations: 43 CFR Part 10, www.law.cornell.edu/cfr/text/43/10 (Accessed 8 July 2013).

Guidelines Cited

Secretary of the Interior's Standards for Rehabilitation, www.nps.gov/tps/standards/rehabilitation/rehab/stand.htm (Accessed 8 July 2013).

Case Law Cited

Comanche Nation v. United States, US Dist. Ct. W. Dist. OK 2008, turtletalk.files.wordpress.com/2008/08/dct-order-granting-tro.pdf (Accessed 6 July 2013).

Navajo Nation v. U.S. Forest Service. 535 F.3d 1058 (9th Cir. 2008), cdn.ca9.uscourts.gov/datastore/opinions/2008/08/07/0615371.pdf (Accessed 9 July 2013).

Pueblo of Sandia v. United States, 50 F.3d 856 (10th Cir. 1995), caselaw.findlaw.com/us-10th-circuit/1051385.html (Accessed 6 July 2013).

Quechan Tribe of the Fort Yuma Reservation v. U.S. Department of the Interior, US Dist. Ct. S. Dist. CA 2010, www.courthousenews.com/2010/12/23/injunction%20tessera.pdf (Accessed 6 July 2013).

Quechan Tribe of the Fort Yuma Reservation v. U.S. Department of the Interior, US Dist. Ct. S. Dist. CA 2013, www.narf.org/nill/bulletins/dct/documents/quechan_feb_27.html (Accessed 6 July 2013).

INDEX

Claudia Nissley, president of Nissley Environmental Consultants, specializes in historic preservation and conservation. She served as the State Historic Preservation Officer at the State of Wyoming Governor's request and was the Director for the West Office of the ACHP with oversight for states and territories west of the Mississippi River and east of Japan. She has worked with American Indian Tribes, government agencies, and others in 40 states. As a national expert in implementation of NHPA, she provides expert testimony, and assistance with consultation and conflict resolution. She presents classes nationally through the National Preservation Institute for five federal environmental and cultural property laws. She may be reached at cnissleyenviro@gmail.com.

Tom King holds a PhD in anthropology, with research in western North America and the Pacific Islands. His career since the late 1960s has been devoted to environmental impact assessment and cultural heritage management, working with government agencies, indigenous communities, and non-governmental organizations. He has authored, co-authored, or edited ten textbooks, numerous journal articles, a novel, and a non-fiction trade book, and writes a blog at crmplus.blogspot.com/. He provides consulting, writing, training, and expert witness services to Indian tribes, government agencies, and private sector clients. He also serves as volunteer senior archaeologist with The International Group for Historic Aircraft Recovery (www.TIGHAR.org), and has published a novel and co-authored a non-fiction book about the group's research into the fates of aviation pioneers Amelia Earhart and Fred Noonan. He can be contacted at tfking106@aol.com.

**green
press**
INITIATIVE